How to Turn Learners On ...
without turning them off

Ways to ignite interest in learning

Third Edition

Robert F. Mager

Books by Robert F. Mager

Preparing Instructional Objectives, *Third Edition**

Measuring Instructional Results, *Third Edition**

Analyzing Performance Problems, *Third Edition**
(with Peter Pipe)

Goal Analysis, *Third Edition**

How to Turn Learners On ... without turning them off, *Third Edition**

Making Instruction Work, *Second Edition**

Developing Vocational Instruction (with Kenneth Beach)

Troubleshooting the Troubleshooting Course

The How to Write a Book Book

What Every Manager Should Know About Training

* Sold as a six-volume set (The Mager Six-Pack)

WORKSHOPS BY ROBERT F. MAGER

Criterion-Referenced Instruction (with Peter Pipe)

Instructional Module Development

The Training Manager Workshop

For more information, contact:
  The Center for Effective Performance, Inc.
  4250 Perimeter Park South, Suite 131
  Atlanta, GA 30341
  (770) 458-4080 or (800) 558-4237

ISBN 1-879-618-18-4 (PREVIOUSLY ISBN 1-56103-337-5)
ISBN 1-879-618-15-X (SIX-VOLUME SET)
Library of Congress Catalog Card Number: 96-72444
Printed in the United States of America

05 04 03 02 01 00 99 98 97   10 9 8 7 6 5 4 3 2 1

Contents

There once was a teacher
Whose principal feature
Was hidden in quite an odd way.
 Students by millions
 Or possibly zillions
 Surrounded him all of the day.

When finally seen
By his scholarly dean
And asked how he managed the deed,
 He lifted three fingers
 And said, "All you swingers
 Need only to follow my lead.

"To rise from a zero
To big Campus Hero,
To answer these questions you'll strive:
 Where am I going,
 How shall I get there, and
 How will I know I've arrived?"

RFM

Preface

ONCE UPON A TIME in a little drop of water, King Amoeba decided he wanted to teach his subjects how to have a better life. So he traveled far and wide throughout the Kingdom of Dropland to tell his people how to be better than they were. But nobody listened.

"Psst," said his adviser. "First you have to get their attention. Here. Rub on this magic garlic potion and you will get everyone's attention."

So the king did as he was told and went out to teach his people how to be better than they were. But nobody listened. They swam away . . . and held their noses.

"Psst," said his adviser. "You have to be sure they can hear you. Here. Shout into this megaphone and then everyone will listen."

So the king did as he was told, and went out to spread his wisdom. But nobody listened. They swam away . . . and held their noses . . . and covered their ears.

"Psst," said his adviser. "The people are too stupid to realize what wisdom you have to offer. You have to *make* them listen for their *own good*."

So the king made everyone gather in the Great Solarium while he told them and told them how to be better than they were. But when the Great Doors were opened, everybody swam away so hard and so fast that before they knew it, they had swum right out of Dropland. And henceforth and forever-more they were referred to as Outdroppers.

And the moral of this fable is that . . . *things surrounded by unpleasantness are seldom surrounded by people.*

There is no question that what we *teach* is often different from what we *tell*. Sometimes we teach the beauty and impor-tance of a subject as well as its substance. Sometimes, though, we teach people to dislike, and then to avoid, the very subject we are teaching them about.

How to Turn Learners On . . . without turning them off is about a universal goal of instruction—the intent to send stu-dents away from instruction with at least as favorable an atti-tude toward the subjects taught as they had when they first arrived. It is about the conditions that influence this attitude, about how to recognize it, and about how to evaluate it.

This book is *not* about what to teach. It is simply about a way to help students get the best use of what they have been taught, and about how to influence them to learn more about your favorite subject after they have left you.

If you care whether your students use what you have taken the trouble to teach them, this book is for you.

Robert F. Mager

Carefree, Arizona
January 1997

Part I

Where Am I Going?

1
What It's All About

A thing, to be useful, has got to be used
But hated things, sir, are less used than abused.

How would you like to be able to organize your instruction so that students become so interested and absorbed in what you're teaching that they try to break down your door to arrive early and hang around until you kick them out of the class-room? How would you like to be able to increase the smile count of your students when they enter your learning area? And most importantly of all, how would you like them to leave your instruction eager to think about, to talk about, and to *apply* what you've taught them?

Does that sound too good to be true?

It isn't. Furthermore, it isn't even very difficult to accomplish. Let me tell you a story.

The year was 1967 when twenty-five thirteen-year-olds were selected to participate in a project designed to improve the education in their district. When the project began in this very poor school district, things couldn't have been much worse. These kids, with IQs ranging from 78 to 104, had significant behavior problems. They seldom came to school, were bored when they did, and dropped out as soon as they could. They hated the curriculum.

Then one day, four project teachers said, in effect, "We're going to throw out this boring school curriculum—and we're going to teach you how to *fly!*" Fly? That got their attention.

Why, most of these kids hadn't been out of the neighborhood in which they were born. But fly? Now *that* was interesting.

And, with the help of local private aviation, they did get to fly. All the students got to "drive" the plane for a few minutes on their very first flight (you don't have to know the history of wings to keep a small plane level), and when they returned to earth, became instant heroes in their neighborhood.

To remain heroes and heroines, they had to stay with the curriculum. But a funny thing happened to that "boring" curriculum. The kids discovered that they had to learn to speak clear English—to communicate with the control tower operators. They had to learn math and map reading—to plan fuel supplies. They had to learn geography—to plot their courses. And they became *interested* in learning these, as well as other, subjects. So interested, that they voluntarily built a wind tunnel in the classroom, and both boys and girls eagerly dove into the engines they were given to disassemble. So interested, in fact, that their behavior problems began to evaporate, their attendance increased, and their grades went up. The result? Forty-four percent of the flight group received honor grades in math in senior high school. And not one student dropped out.

"Gosh," you might be thinking. "*We* couldn't do anything like *that*. Where would we get an airplane?" (Actually, that was the easiest part; industry would just love to have an opportunity to provide assistance with projects that make sense.) But it wouldn't take airplanes to get the same sort of results. The teachers could just as easily have said, "We're going to teach you all to be motion picture directors." Or firefighters. Or police officers. Or software developers. Or race-car drivers. Or any of several other things of high interest to students. In each case the students' interest in learning the "boring" subjects of the typical curriculum would increase. Eagerness to learn would improve because the subjects of that curriculum would suddenly have meaning.

There are many similar stories that could be told about how an attitude toward learning was kindled and fanned into a flame so bright that students became not only eager to learn, but eager to apply their learning in the world around them.

You can do it, too; that's what this book is about.

- It's about what you can do to send your students away with a stronger interest in your subject than when they arrived.
- It's about how to send them away not only willing, but eager, to apply what you've taught them.
- And it's about how to avoid sending them away with less interest in your subject than when they arrived.

The Plot

Because the concept of attitudes is an abstraction (a fuzzy) open to several interpretations, we'll need to learn how to say exactly what we mean when we say that our goal is to inspire a favorable attitude toward learning in our students.

Having clarified our perception of what attitudes are, we'll be in a position to describe the attitude outcomes we might be interested in achieving.

Next, we'll learn to recognize approach and avoidance responses (those that indicate favorable or unfavorable attitudes). This skill will help us to recognize progress toward our goals.

Then, because attitudes are shaped, in part, by the conditions and consequences that surround the student attempting to learn, we'll need to explore which of those conditions and consequences work in our favor and which work against us.

By then you'll be ready to learn about a powerful way to make sure that those who *do* have favorable attitudes will actually be willing to put their knowledge and skills into practice with enough confidence to persevere in the face of obstacles and setbacks.

Finally, we'll consider ways to assess the results of our efforts; that is, ways to find out how well we're doing turning our students on, rather than off.

So let's do it.

2

Why It's All About

If telling were the same as teaching,
we'd all be so smart we could hardly stand it.

Why do we teach? Why do we go to the trouble of analyzing, designing, developing, and delivering instruction? What do we hope to accomplish by these efforts?

Don't we instruct because we hope that through our instruction our students will somehow be *different* than they were before the instruction? Don't we teach in order to increase the capabilities of our students?

Consider any of the instruction you yourself may have given. Why did you coach, or tutor, or otherwise assist students to learn? Wasn't it because you hoped they would, as a result of your efforts,

- know more than they knew before?
- understand something they did not understand before?
- develop a skill that was not developed before?
- feel differently about a subject than they felt before?
- develop an appreciation for something where there was little or none before?

If your intent *wasn't* to achieve one or more of these goals, then what in the world were you doing it for?

If they were no different as a result of the instruction, there might have been teaching—but there was no learning. Unless students are changed in some way by the instruction, the instruction cannot be regarded as successful.

Important as that is, it's not enough. After all, we don't go to the bother of teaching just so that students will be able to demonstrate their competence during, or at the end of, the instruction—just so they can go away saying, "Well, that's that. I hope I never hear of *that* subject again. Now I can get on with other things." We want them to go away saying favorable things about the subject and about what they've learned. More, we want them to be willing, and even eager, to actually apply what they've learned in the world around them.

Thus, our primary concern is with influencing how students are able to perform *after* the course is over, *after* our influence is discontinued. We try to instill an appreciation for music now so that students will behave appreciatively *after* our help has been withdrawn. We try to teach them to read, to calculate, to analyze *now* so that they will be able to do those things in the *future*. And whether we are concerned with performance in the immediate future or in the more remote future, we are concerned that our teaching influence become at least as evident *then* as we want it to become evident *now*.

Certainly one of the important goals of education is that the influence of an educational experience will extend beyond the period of instruction. Put another way, we teach so that our students will be able and willing to do something *at some time after our direct influence has ended.* If it's worth teaching, it's worth working toward having that teaching put to use.

How?

There are many things that we can do to influence student attitude toward learning and toward the application of that learning. Some of those things have to do with how the instructional materials are constructed and arranged; some, with how they are presented to the student; some, with what happens to students as they are learning; and some, with what happens to them as a result of their efforts.

Instructors, of course, don't control *all* of the factors that influence attitude toward learning. There are parents, peers, and neighborhoods. There are bosses, corporate policies, and laws. There is the uncle who was admired and the aunt who was there to show the way. And then, of course, there is the mass media.

But we can't pass the buck; we can't avoid facing the responsibility that flows from the fact that *we* influence attitude toward learning. The fact that there are other sources of influence doesn't alter the fact that instructors, as a group, constitute one of those sources. Since this is the case, it is up to each instructor to take whatever steps are available to assure that his or her influence is constructive rather than destructive. But how much does it matter? To answer that, let's try a little metaphor:

Let's Suppose

Let's suppose that everyone in the world had a balloon growing out of his or her head, and let's suppose that the size of the balloon represented the strength of its owner's self-esteem. A larger balloon would mean that its owner had a strong and healthy self-concept, while a smaller balloon would mean that the self-concept was in poor condition.

And let's suppose that as people wend their way through life, their balloons would expand and shrivel in response to the situations they encounter and in response to the things that happen to them. When they find themselves in a situation that is pleasant or nurturing, their balloons would expand. When the results of their efforts lead to a warm or positive feeling, once again their balloons would expand. But each time they met with an unpleasant (aversive) consequence, such as humiliation or embarrassment, their balloons would shrivel just a bit. Many such experiences would shrivel their balloons to nearly empty.

Now, if *you* met someone with a shriveled balloon, you, being a good person, might go out of your way to say or do something intended to help that sickly balloon to expand. And, since you could actually see the state of that person's psyche, you would probably be careful not to do or say anything that would shrivel it even further. At the very least, you might be more thoughtful about how you treated that person and about how you phrased your comments. Rather than barge in with, "Hey. Your fly's unzipped. Are you advertising?" you would probably think about how to communicate this information in a more private and emotionally neutral way.

Now, if we could actually *see* the condition of everyone's self-esteem, and if we could *see* the results of our own words and actions on their balloons, we would quickly learn how to become better at expanding and to avoid shriveling. And we would probably avoid ways of saying things that offend or humiliate others and replace them with words that made them feel better about themselves. In fact, one of the goals of becoming a "better person" might be that of minimizing our shriveling effect and maximizing our expanding effect on those we influence . . . especially on those we care about.

And because it would make *you* feel good when you could see that you had done something to expand someone else's balloon, your *own* balloon would grow as well.

But we can't actually see the size of someone else's balloon, can we? It's all hidden away inside the person. And "hidden" is the right word, because people often work hard to hide the size of their balloons from the eyes of others. You know the words that tell you this is true: "Put on a happy face," "Keep a stiff upper lip," and "Don't wear your emotions on your sleeve." And when we're being polite, or acting like ladies and gentlemen, or being tactful, it is often our intention to hide the shriveling effects that someone else's thoughtless words and acts may have on *us.*

So what to do? After all, we know that whether or not we can see their balloons, our own actions serve to make them grow or shrivel. And we know that our actions affect others whether we intend it or not. We know because the laws of nature tell us so.

So what to do? How can we ensure that we are among the expanders and among those who are expanded in return? And how can we avoid being the shrivelers of others and therefore avoid being shriveled in return?

Since we *know* that our actions affect others, and since we *know* there are laws of nature that influence the strength of this effect, the answer lies in becoming adept at accentuating the positive and eliminating the negative.

The answer lies in learning to recognize, and to apply, those natural laws (principles) in ways that will lead to favorable, rather than to unfavorable—or random—results.

That's why it matters that we take all available steps to make sure that we are expanders, rather than shrivelers, of personal balloons.

Summary So Far

- *Learning is for the* future; *that is, the object of instruction is to facilitate some form of behavior at a point after the instruction has been completed.*

- *People influence people. Teachers, and others,* do *influence attitudes toward subject matter and toward learning itself, whether they want to or not.*

- *One goal toward which to strive is to have students leave your influence with their attitudes as favorable as possible toward your subject. In this way you will maximize the like- lihood that students will be willing to use what they have learned and will be willing to learn more about what they have been taught.*

And Now?

We'll begin by exploring the concept of attitude. A certain amount of confusion usually surrounds this topic, and we'll need to sort it out before we can get down to business.

3
Defining the Goal

If you're not sure where you're going,
you're likely to end up somewhere else.

Although goals such as "provide good customer service," "appreciate democracy," or "have a favorable attitude toward learning" may be laudable, they are difficult—if not impossible—to achieve when stated in such vague terms. They mean different things—quite possibly equally valid different things—to different people. Though these goals may *name* an important intention, they do not provide us with any information about what the intention would look like if achieved. And if we don't know what successful goal achievement looks like, we have no clues about what to do to accomplish that success. Before proceeding to action, therefore, we must spend a little time thinking about, and describing, the results we expect to achieve.

Let's consider the word "attitude." Although "attitude" is a useful word in everyday conversation—and I have used it myself earlier in this book—it is about as useful as a boot in a bedpan when we are serious about strengthening a favorable attitude.

So let's think about attitude.

Is attitude a thing?

Wellll, no . . . attitude isn't a thing like a nose or a noose. You couldn't dissect a person's favorable attitude toward gumdrops and say, "Aha, madam. *There* is your attitude. Allow me to polish it up just a bit."

But if attitude isn't a thing, what is it?

It's a word. Unfortunately, it's a word that has almost as many meanings as there are people using the word. But there is some agreement about the meaning; no matter what the specifics of the meaning are, people who talk about an attitude are almost always talking about a tendency to behave in one way rather than in another. For example, if we note that a clump of people tend to say "Bleaaaugh!" whenever they are faced with limp string beans, we might conclude that they don't like limp string beans. We might say that they have an unfavorable attitude toward those mushy things. If we note that another gaggle of people tend to fall asleep shortly after the after-dinner speech begins, we might conclude that they have an unfavorable attitude about speakers. It is important to note that whenever we make such observations, we are making inferences *based on visible behavior.*

As a matter of fact, *all* statements about attitude are based on circumstantial evidence: on the evidence of what people say and do.

A good friend of mine has a favorable attitude toward Bach; that is, he likes to listen to music written by Bach. Now this statement is an inference on my part about a tendency, inclination, propensity—or "attitude." It is a conclusion about a general state of affairs based on circumstantial evidence. What kind of circumstantial evidence? Well, he talks about Bach whenever he can slip him into a conversation, and he frequently locates himself where the music of Bach is being played. And he does this for no reason at all . . . by which I mean there is no observable coercion. He simply makes numerous "moving toward" responses to Bach's music. So, from my observations I infer that he has a positive attitude toward Bach.

Attitude Statements Are Predictions. Whenever we make statements about attitudes, we are making predictions about the future behavior of people based on our observations of past behavior. Our predictions, or conclusions, may be right or wrong; but they are predictions nonetheless.

When I say that my friend has a favorable attitude toward Bach, for example, I not only base that statement on things he has said and done in the past, I also predict what that means in the future. I predict that he will take every possible opportunity to put himself into the presence of Bach-like things. I predict he will listen to the music, play it on his piano, go to concerts, etc. If we say that someone has a favorable attitude toward customers, we predict (expect) that rather than avoid customers, this person would approach them, smile at them, ask how he or she may be helpful, provide assistance, and so on.

On the other hand, if we say that someone has a negative attitude about scorpions, we are predicting that this person would avoid the beasties whenever possible, would pass up opportunities to have one as a pet, and would say negative rather than positive things about them.

When we tag someone as having a "favorable attitude," we are predicting some form of *moving toward* responses, and this prediction is based on some "moving toward" behavior already seen. Conversely, tagging a person as having a "negative attitude" is predicting *moving away from* responses, and that prediction is based on some "moving away from" behavior already observed.

Our quest, then, is to increase the strength of approach tendencies toward the subject and to minimize the strength of avoidance tendencies toward the subject; it is to cause the subject to become the object of "moving toward" behaviors rather than of "moving away from" behaviors.

Specifically, we have two goals:

1. Students will exhibit at least as strong an approach tendency (favorable attitude) toward the subject of _____ when they leave your influence as they had when they arrived.

2. When students leave your influence they will be willing to apply what they have learned to the world around them.

These are our goals. And because they should be our primary goals regardless of what we are teaching, or whom we are teaching, they can be referred to as universal goals. No matter what else we accomplish, or fail to accomplish, with our instruction, we should do no harm to student attitude toward learning— and attitude toward what we are teaching.

And Now?

Before we can decide what actions to take to increase an approach tendency (favorable attitude) and decrease an avoidance tendency (unfavorable attitude), we need to be sure we can recognize approach and avoidance responses when we see or hear them. That's what we'll do next.

Part II

How Shall I Get There?

4

Recognizing Approach and Avoidance

A teacher with insight once turned
To a colleague and said, "I've discerned
That if I'm aversive
While waxing discursive
My students detest what
they've learned."

R.F.M.

I'd rather be fishing," says one bumper sticker; "I'd rather be sailing," says another. Both are announcing a preference for one activity over others; both are announcing an approach tendency. Given a choice of activities, those bumper stick*ors* are telling us they would choose fishing and sailing over other activities. And the acts of obtaining and gluing the stickers to the bumpers are examples of approach responses.

Approach Responses

An approach response is an action that indicates a moving

toward an object, activity, or situation. It is a behavior that attempts to get the behaver closer to the target of the approach. It is a behavior that indicates an affinity for the subject of the approach, whether that be sailing, mathematics, or asparagus.

There are several ways in which you could demonstrate an approach tendency. For example, you could physically move toward the target of your affinity (hoping you won't get slapped for moving too close). You could speak favorably about the subject. You could encourage others to become interested in the subject. You could spend time "fondling" or caressing the subject, as people often do when curled up with a good book or when working on a favorite car.

The world around us is filled with approach responses, and a little practice in observation will quickly enable you to spot them by the dozens. To get you started, let's consider some examples from a variety of areas.

Baseball Fans

First, let's take a look at a baseball fan. I'm sure you'll agree that fans have strong approach tendencies toward the target of their fanniness, and that they exhibit any number of behaviors indicating their liking of their favorite activity.

What tells you that someone likes baseball? What does he or she do that causes you to conclude that this person is nuts about the sport?

Suppose you were to observe a fan for a week, and suppose you were to record in your notebook everything he or she did that you consider evidence of a liking for baseball. At the end of the week, your notes might read something like this:

- Talks incessantly about baseball.
- Reads every word about the subject printed on the sports page of both local newspapers.

- Can recite the batting averages of all players of all teams in both leagues.
- During the observation week, watched every game telecast.
- On Tuesday and Thursday, risked losing his or her job by calling in sick in order to attend doubleheaders.
- On Friday, infuriated his or her spouse by watching baseball during a dinner party.
- On Saturday, infuriated his or her spouse by spending the "dinner-out" money on the baseball pool.

This list by no means exhausts the possibilities. You will be astonished at the number of approach responses you will find once you begin to look for them. Some time ago, I ran into an excellent example of approach response toward this very subject. In a letter to one of the personal-advice columns of the old Chicago *Daily News,* a woman wrote:

"I know men are crazy about sports, but my husband carries this too far. He even took a radio to his sister's wedding so he wouldn't miss the baseball game."

Clearly this man's behavior was intended to cause him to come closer to, or to remain in contact longer with, the subject of baseball; it is an approach response.

Opera Buffs

Next, consider the person who is known as an "opera enthusiast." If you were to observe and record this individual's behavior for a while to see what might have led to such a description, your notes might look something like this:

- Attended all local operas, regardless of cost.
- Talked about opera at length whenever possible.

- Told non-enthusiasts that they "just don't know what they are missing."
- Read books about opera.
- Frequently hums arias from various operas.
- Subscribes to an opera magazine.
- Owns an extensive record collection of favorite operas.

Again, the list of responses that represent an attempt to approach or remain in contact with opera has not been exhausted. Can you think of others?

Enthusiastic Students

Now let's look for approach responses more closely related to instruction. Here's an individual currently enrolled in the second semester of a college biology course. The student's instructor is frequently referred to as "enthusiastic," "inspiring," and "a good teacher." But you don't want to ask about the behavior of the instructor at this point. You are interested in the behavior of the student; more specifically, in discovering evidence from which to predict the nature of this student's future behavior toward the subject of biology. A week-long observation of this student might reveal the following:

- During the week, student went to the library twelve times; used 70 percent of the time spent there reading biology books.
- Tuesday evening, student attended meeting of the university biology club; broke date to attend.
- Wednesday morning, spent $100 on biology texts and dissecting instruments.
- Survey of attendance records shows that student has never missed a biology lecture or laboratory but has cut two or three classes in each of several other courses.

- During the week's three lectures and two laboratory periods, student asked 14 questions, all related to biology.
- Asked to see the course instructor twice in office appointments to discuss points not covered in the course.
- On Thursday, student crouched on the banks of a river for three pre-dawn hours to capture frogs for use as lab specimens.
- Student met with adviser and asked to register for an advanced biology course.

You may object that this list contains exaggerations or that there are omissions, and you may not be willing to accept all the items as relevant to your own situation, but you will surely agree that it contains responses that can be used to make predictions (statements of approach or avoidance tendencies) about the student's future behavior toward biology.

Self-Paced Learners

The biology course just discussed had a lecture format. Let's look at a few of the approach responses commonly seen in courses operated according to a format that is both self-paced and criterion-referenced (competency-based). In these courses, students are given a copy of the course objectives so they know exactly what they must learn to do to be considered competent. They are given a variety of resources from which to learn and practice and are given a great deal of decision-making power over their own instruction. Instructors are available as coaches who assist whenever they are needed. Here are some of the approach behaviors you are likely to see in such a course setting. The students:

- Fix work that is not yet adequate, without urging or pressure.

- Spend time with colleagues (other students) discussing their work or reviewing the colleagues' work.
- Complete more practice exercises than required.
- Come early and stay late.
- Sign up other people at their company for the course.

At one competency-based course in which managers and their team members learn some elements of modern management practice,[1] a number of students were so enthusiastic about what they were learning that they appointed themselves as a task force charged with implementing the techniques of management by objectives back at their organization. They held meetings on their own and developed an action plan. In addition, they drafted and rehearsed a presentation to be made to an executive vice-president upon their return to the company. Finally, they all asked their bosses to be allowed to become certified course managers (instructors) of the course. Strong evidence of approach? You bet.

A word about "comes early/stays late" before moving on. Instructors of lecture courses often complain that students don't get to class on time. Instructors of self-paced, competency-based courses, on the other hand, often mumble about students who want to show up at 7:00 a.m. and who don't want to leave at the end of the workshop day. In our own courses,[2] we have had to establish a policy of simply leaving the students at 4:30 p.m. and going to another room to complete our daily debriefing. Even so, many students continue to work at their learning projects until the doors are locked at 6:00 p.m. This may sound unlikely to you if you have

---

[1] *Blueprint for Performance®*, Fourth Edition, a workshop course on performance management, created by Bonnie MacLean Abney (Abney International, Sebastopol, CA, 1994, 1979).

[2] *CRI (Criterion-Referenced Instruction): Practical Skills for Design Instruction that Works,* Fourth Edition, by R.F. Mager and Peter Pipe (The Center for Effective Performance, Atlanta, GA, 1994).

never experienced this form of instruction; I can assure you, however, that it is not an unusual experience for those who operate their courses in this fashion. In Duluth, Minnesota, for example, soon after the public schools went to a competency-based format, teachers' complaints changed from "We can't get them to show up on time," to "We can't get them to go home in the afternoon." You understand the reason for the complaint— if there are students on the premises, there has to be a teacher there as well.

As you can see by these examples, people who are strongly disposed toward a subject talk a great deal about it, encourage others to participate in it, read about it, buy books about it, study it, publish papers about it, and enter careers about it. Students strongly disposed toward a subject sign up for more courses about it, say favorable things about it, and spend time practicing it.

In general, then, we can say that people with strong approach tendencies toward a subject keep coming back for more experiences with the subject. They seek out experiences with the subject in preference to other desirable experiences. *The more strongly they are attracted to a subject, the more obstacles they will overcome to come into contact with it and stay in contact with it.**

Identifying vs. Weighing

There is a difference between recognizing a thing and putting weight or value on it. It's one thing to say, "That's a stone," and another to say, "That stone weighs five pounds." The same is true for approach and avoidance responses. Identifying them is not the same as interpreting and weighing

---

* One of the most interesting examples of an approach response was this classified advertisement brought to my attention by Peter Pipe:
WANTED: Someone who watches *Love of Life* to fill in an episode missed.

them. Some are stronger indicators of approach, or avoidance, and others are weaker. No matter, as long as you remember that the goal is to maximize the incidence of approach behaviors and minimize the incidence of avoidance behaviors.

Avoidance Responses

Approach tendencies, however, are only half the story. There are also activities that some people tend to avoid. If we can identify responses that lead us to conclude that a person favors an activity or a subject, we should also be able to identify responses indicating a person's tendency to avoid it.

Consider this pithy dialogue:

"Ahh, kiss me, you fool."
"Thank you, but I'd rather not."
"Why not?"
"I never kiss on Wednesdays."

It seems fairly obvious that the second speaker is trying to move away from the first speaker. This is an avoidance response, even though it is verbal. It does not matter *why* the behavior occurred. It doesn't matter whether it was because the first speaker suffered from bad breath or from crumpled toes. It doesn't matter whether it had anything to do with the attraction, or lack of it, of the second speaker for the first. If the response was "moving away from" behavior, it was an avoidance response.

Had you been observing and recording my behavior during the time I was working on the revision of this chapter, your notes might have looked something like this:

- Turned on word processor and typewriter.
- Got up to sharpen pencil.

- Straightened pile of papers.
- Watched bunnies cavorting in desert outside window.
- Typed half a page.
- Watched covey of baby quail stroll by.
- Got up to check thermometer.

Some of those responses look like approach responses and others like avoidance. Whatever my excuse or explanation, those that took me farther away from writing can be called avoidance responses. (I dunno about you, but I find writing to be hard work.)

There are some subjects that may be avoided by people who actually "like" them very much. A dieter, for example, might manage to say, "No, thank you," when offered a favorite dish, or a spendthrift might resist buying coveted new clothes. These are special cases where someone avoids doing something in order to avoid an even more aversive (undesirable or disagreeable) consequence. The dieter avoids getting heavier and more uncomfortable (and possibly, avoids some stern comments from his or her physician); the spendthrift avoids getting a bill that he or she can't afford to pay.

But what about matters closer to the classroom—actions that might be used to infer an avoidance tendency toward an academic subject? The record of a student in his or her second semester of a required college mathematics course might look like this:

- On Tuesday, student tried to persuade mathematics instructor to excuse him or her from the course.
- Student failed to turn in three of four mathematics assignments on time.
- On Wednesday, student spoke with adviser about dropping out of mathematics course.
- On Monday and Wednesday, student was late for mathematics class; on Friday, student failed to appear.

- Told everyone possible that math was useless in the real world and a waste of time to learn.

What other evidence of avoidance have you seen while attending someone else's course? Ever seen these? Ever seen the students:

- Show up late?
- Show up for class unprepared (no paper, no writing tools, etc.)?
- Say unfavorable things about the subject of the course or about the instructional procedures?
- Daydream?
- Disrupt the class?
- Try to discourage others from signing up for the course?
- Try to get by without practicing or studying?

What else can you add? What else have you seen people do, or heard them say, that suggested they would rather avoid contact with the subject, or with the instruction itself, or with the learning, or with the instructor?

What? "SMATs 'n' SMUTs"?

I had an opportunity to witness a hilarious assortment of avoidance behaviors during the original drafting of this book. Since the book was to be about Subject Matter Approach Tendencies, and in a way about Subject Matter Unapproach Tendencies, I referred to the book around the house as "SMATs 'n' SMUTs." When my wife or kids would ask me what I was working on, I'd reply, "Oh, I'm trying to make some progress on 'SMATs 'n' SMUTs.'"

As that became the "name" of the book around the house, I suggested it to the publisher as a title for the book. Well! You wouldn't believe the anguish this caused. Had you been watching, you would have heard and seen the following:

- Publisher recovers from shock and says, "There, there, now (pat, pat), that's a nice little joke ... but you aren't *serious?*"
- Publisher suggests list of alternate titles.
- Editor says, "Well, let's see if it fits after we've worked through the rest of it," hoping it would go away.
- Editor launches into heart-rending lament about the *Fanny Hill* implications of the title, and about how publishing people have a better "feel" for titles (and everything else) than authors.
- Editor melts into a little puddle.

In the face of such grief and pathos, I naturally gave up and settled for a phootnote. Imagine my surprise when, during the crafting of the second edition, the *editor* suggested that we use "SMATs 'n' SMUTs" as a subtitle. What had happened to cause the change of heart? The fact that catchy subtitles are used by readers more often than titles? The fact that readers suggested using it as the main title? An emboldening of the spirit? A mellowing of the psyche? Whatever the cause, there was a gradual transition from avoidance to approach (which should tell you that it is possible to change avoidance to approach).

Meanwhile, back to the subject at hand. Given a choice, people with avoidance tendencies elect to approach something *other* than the subject in question. They will go to varying lengths to prevent contact with the subject. They do not buy or read books about the subject, they do not join clubs relating to the subject, and they do not seek out discussions concerning the subject. When they are faced with the subject, they act to move away from it by changing the topic of conversation, by walking away from the stimulus, or by inventing an excuse to avoid the subject or terminate contact with it.

More importantly, in instructional situations, people often verbalize a conviction that they cannot learn a particular subject matter and that they intend to have as little as possible to do with the subject in the future. *Once such a behavior pattern develops, it is unlikely that they will put themselves in situations where the attitude is likely to be reversed.*

To the extent students avoid experiences with a subject, they will have fewer opportunities to change their avoidance tendencies to approach tendencies. In addition, if students avoid experiences with a subject, it is improbable that they will use, and therefore maintain, whatever skill they had, and almost certain that they will be less willing to learn more about it as time goes by. Each subject that students avoid constitutes the loss of a tool or skill that might have eased their journey through a complex world.

It is for this reason that instruction that teaches students to avoid learning and applying a subject does the student more harm than good.

That good intentions are not enough was clearly demonstrated by an approach/avoidance analysis I conducted for a high-school teacher of mathematics. This teacher is highly motivated to generate enthusiasm and appreciation for mathematics in her students. She likes what she teaches and is anxious that her students share her excitement for the subject. She is courteous and respectful of student questions and makes herself available for questions.

But in spite of her intentions and her initial success at motivation, she managed to *reduce* math interest in about as many students as she managed to increase it.

How? What could such a teacher be doing to diminish subject matter approach tendencies?

It was a classic example of "overkill." She inadvertently spent a great deal of class time presenting material beyond the ability of her students to understand. Her enthusiasm for her subject caused her to try to teach almost everything she knew about math, and that was a lot more than students could understand, regardless of how motivated they were to try. Some students concluded that they could never understand math, and they lost interest.

How to Identify Approach/Avoidance Responses

Here are three procedures that will help you to improve your ability to pinpoint approach and avoidance responses:

1. Think of something that your best friend likes, or dislikes, and ask yourself what that friend *does* or *says* that causes you to conclude that he or she has that like or dislike.

2. When you hear someone say something like "They have a poor attitude toward_____," or "They are strongly motivated to_____," ask that person "What do they say or do that causes you to make that comment about their attitude or motivation?"

3. Carry a small notebook and note each event that leads you to believe that a student is either favorably or unfavorably disposed toward the subject you are teaching. This will help you to get into the habit of observing and identifying clues to approach and avoidance.

The Procedure

The ability to recognize approach and avoidance responses is the key for getting more of the first and less of the second. But how? Here's the procedure. Briefly, the procedure asks you to:

- describe the approach responses you value,
- find out where things stand at present, and then
- take steps to eliminate the negative and accentuate the positive.

In practice, this procedure looks like this:

1. Decide what approach responses you value and write them down. You must have a visible list before you can complete the other steps. For example, do you want your students to:

   - arrive prepared to work (i.e., with books, manuals, notebooks, pencils, or other equipment)?
   - begin working on the instruction next in line for study?
   - practice the material being learned?
   - willingly correct work that is not yet adequate?
   - speak favorably about the subject?
   - ask for discussions about related aspects of the subject?
   - ask questions when the instruction is unclear?
   - do more work than necessary?
   - discuss the subject with other students?
   - spend time actually performing the skills being learned?

These are only sample items that might be useful in getting your own list started.

2. Check each item on your list to make sure it is reasonable and makes sense. Are these responses that you can observe? Do they represent reasonable expectations (i.e., are you expecting more than they can reasonably be expected to deliver)? When your list is complete (for now), then

3. Determine the extent to which each of the responses is occurring to your satisfaction now. That is, find out where things stand in relation to each of the items on your list. How? Ask people, use questionnaires, count the

number of people who make the desired responses, and so on. I'll have more to say on this topic in a later chapter.

4. Focus on one avoidance response you would like to eliminate, or an approach response you would like to strengthen, and take the appropriate action (to be described in Chapter 5).

Once you have a visible picture of what you expect your students to do—whether that doing is related to approach/avoidance or something else—you will be ready to think about ways to accentuate the positive and eliminate the negative. We'll do that next.

5

Sources of Influence

If our actions didn't sometimes shout louder than our words, there would be no call for the expression, "Don't do as I do, do as I say."

A while ago, Von Haney, a talented graphic artist, created a short animation sequence for an instructional program designed to teach mothers how to increase their success at interaction with those around them. In this scene there are two small boys, one empty-handed and the other holding and sucking a huge lollipop. The empty-handed boy speaks first:

"Hi. Where'd you get the sucker?"

"My mommy gave it to me—as a reward for crying."

"You mean your mommy *wants you* to cry?"

"I guess so. Whenever I cry she gives me a lollipop."

"Gee, I'd cry a *lot* more often if I always got a sucker."

"Of course. It's elementary psychology!"

Most people who have seen this scene just *know* there was something wrong with the way the mother went about trying to reduce crying, although they are often unable to put their finger on exactly what went awry. The sequence makes it obvious that crying behavior is not reduced by following it with a lollipop. But why not? Though the scene doesn't tell us any of the details, it certainly does suggest that there are more successful and less successful ways of interacting and influencing others.

The business/industry version of the lollipop dialogue goes something like this:

"Hey! How'd you get the trip to Paris?"

"My boss gave it to me—as a reward for screwing up."

"You mean your boss *wants you* to screw up?"

"I guess so. Every time my European operation doesn't meet its production schedules, she sends me to Paris."

Sound unlikely? Not at all. It happens every day; if not in these words, then in others.

"Charlie, you did such a good job on that report, I'm going to give you all the *tough* ones from now on. You're just the man for the job."

Would anyone be surprised to hear that Charlie's lost his steam? That he seems less motivated than he used to be? Suppose you had worked hard on an assignment and were then ignored when you presented the results. Worse, suppose you were asked, "Is *that* the best you can do?" Do you think that would affect how you went about completing the next assignment? Do you think your work would be affected if you never found out how well you were doing, or if you were in some way made to feel smaller as a result of your efforts?

The same holds true for students. They, too, are influenced by the things that happen to them. No one is exempt from the laws of nature.

A few years ago a colleague and I implemented a study designed to chart the history of some tendencies toward, and away from, some academic subjects. We interviewed 65 students, currently enrolled in one course or another, who were all adults and who had completed high school and/or college.

The first questions of the interview were designed to identify the most-favored and the least-favored academic subject of each person. Once these subjects were identified, each person was asked a series of questions to determine just how these inclinations got to be that way. These questions were designed to explore each person's feelings about his or her most-preferred and least-preferred subjects and to determine what the individual remembered as the conditions leading to those feelings, as well as to changes in those feelings.

The results of the study were interesting and somewhat unexpected. Almost every person was able to identify the subjects or school activities that were at the top and at the bottom of his or her "popularity scale." What was unexpected were the responses to the questions attempting to discover why and how these subjects came to be rated as they were.

With regard to *favorite* academic subjects, the interviewees discussed the subjects with some facility; that is, they talked as though they remembered something of the subjects. But they seemed to have no clear idea of how they got to be their favorite subjects. Though they always had an answer to the question "How did it get to be that way?" their answers reflected only vague memories. "Oh, I always liked history," they would say, or, "I was born with an interest in art."

When asked about the subject they liked least, however, the story was different. They seemed to remember little about the subject itself and would often come right out and say, "I don't remember a thing about_____, and the less I hear of it, the better." But they *always* remembered just how they learned to dislike the subject . . . at least they *said* they remembered. They were quite capable of pinpointing the events or conditions that they felt were behind their desire to avoid the subject whenever they could. We were perfectly aware that some of the interviewees had faulty memories. What we were looking for, however, were the conditions and consequences they remembered as having an effect, whether or not they were correct, so we would know what they *said* to other people about the subjects they came to like and dislike.

As you read the sampling of interview summaries that follows, dip back into your own academic history to see if you can add other conditions and consequences that may influence approach and avoidance responses toward subjects taught in school.

Case 1

Favorite subject:	Music.
How it got that way:	I've always liked music. It was just a personal liking. No events had anything to do with it.
Least-favored subject:	English.
How it got that way:	None of the teachers could get down to a level where the students could understand what they were trying to get across. They didn't know how to make the subject interesting.

Case 2

Favorite subject: Art, in high school; psychology, in college.

How it got that way: I've always liked art. Mother encouraged art by providing lots of materials. In high school the instructor was very good. Had a good sense of humor and worked *with* students. He encouraged us to participate in contests. I still use my art knowledge in my work.

Least-favored subject: Mathematics.

How it got that way: I was skipped to third grade after completing only half of second grade. I missed considerable background and felt lost. The third-grade teacher was very impatient and did not believe in individual instruction. She ridiculed me in front of the class. I was above average in all other subjects, but I failed accounting in college.

Case 3

Favorite subject:	History.
How it got that way:	I hated math, wasn't good in English, and so, drifted into history. History interest continued through high school, which is as far as I went. I can't remember anything else that influenced my interest in history, but to this day I continue to study the subject as a hobby.
Least-favored subject:	Mathematics.
How it got that way:	I never could add 2 and 2 and still can't. I changed schools 18 times between first grade and the end of high school. Every time I got to a school, they were studying something for which I had no background, or they were learning something I already knew. Also, there was a grade-school teacher who embarrassed me to death. The instructor once caught me counting on my fingers and took me up to the front of the class to make an example of me. It was humiliating. I hated math.

Case 4

Favorite subject:	Spanish.
How it got that way:	High-school instructor was tremendous; she spoke Spanish from the first day and taught class to sing Spanish songs. She encouraged special projects and allowed better students to help slower ones.
Least-favored subject:	None. (No strong avoidance tendencies toward any subject. In college, this person majored in science. There were two reasons for this: (1) A cousin was taking science and interested the student by talking enthusiastically and by showing homework and experiments. (2) Student had a high-school teacher who had well-organized lectures and a good lab. This instructor checked lab work frequently and showed relevant films and videos that were highly interesting. This instructor was a person to whom students felt they could go with problems. This is an instance where the attitude toward a subject changed over a period of time as the result of events and consequences.)

Case 5

Favorite subject:	Psychology.
How it got that way:	I had a great admiration for the instructor and felt the course was well presented. He did not become angry when students disagreed with him . . . he was willing to be criticized. He did not ridicule. He encouraged his students and had no discipline problems.
Least-favored subject:	Physics.
How it got that way:	I felt I didn't have the mind for it. Also, I had a high-school instructor I liked, but he merely read the text-book to the class and then assigned problems without giving the necessary information that would help in solving them. This instructor couldn't make himself understood.

Summarizing the results of this study, we can say that a favorite subject gets to be that way because the student:

- was comfortable in the presence of the subject.
- admired someone who was competent in the subject or who enjoyed demonstrating or working with the subject.
- found his or her world getting somehow brighter as a result of working with the subject.

A least-favorite subject tends to get that way because the student:

- seems to have little aptitude for it (or feels that way).
- associates the subject with disliked individuals.
- associates the subject with unpleasant circumstances.
- found his or her world getting somehow dimmer as a result of the contact with the subject.

There is no question about the fact that attitudes toward a subject are influenced by factors *other* than those present in the instructional environment. Peers, friends, bosses, and television are just a few of those factors. Our concern, though, is not with whether instructors are the *sole* source of influence, but with whether they are a *positive* source of influence. In other words, if a student is led toward an unfavorable attitude about something being taught, let it not be because of the actions of the instructor or because of the environment created by the instructor.

Try It; You'll Like It

Here's an activity that is always helpful in reminding us of the experiences that cause attitudes toward, and away from, a subject or activity. It follows the study that involved the case just described.

1. First, ask a friend to tell you what his or her favorite and least-favorite school subjects were.

2. Second, ask him or her to tell you how those subjects came to be liked or disliked.

3. Third, ask if your friend has taken a course since starting his or her present job. (Perhaps it was a three-day workshop, a seminar, or a longer course.) If so, ask how your friend felt about that course or seminar.

4. Fourth, ask *why* your friend feels a particular way about this on-the-job course; that is, ask him or her to describe the events that shaped this attitude.

5. Finally, ask yourself this question: "What are the similarities and differences between the attitude-shaping events that occurred in school courses and those that occurred in courses taken while on the job?" Could the events leading to a less-than-positive attitude have been avoided?

Summary

To summarize, sources of influence to approach or avoid subject matter or activities include:

1. *The* conditions *that surround a subject or activity; that is, the conditions that exist while the student is in the presence of, or in contact with, the subject matter or activity.*

2. *The* consequences *of being in the presence of, or coming into contact with, the subject matter or activity; that is, the things that happen as a result of working with the subject.*

3. *The way that others react toward a subject; that is, the attitude* modeled *by others.*

Coming Attractions

Now that we have identified some of the sources of influence, the next step will be to explore just how these sources operate. We'll explore how they should be arranged in order to achieve a desired result.

6
Conditions and Consequences

*Exhortation is used more and accomplishes
less than almost any behavior-changing
tool known to man.*

Three sets of principles which, for our purposes, influence
attitude toward learning are conditions, consequences, and
modeling. So far, so good. But the nature of the conditions, the
way in which consequences are organized, and the way in
which the modeling is done make a difference. When principles are improperly applied, they don't work. Consider this
improbable dialogue:

He: Y'know, I tried that gravity stuff.
She: You did?
He: Yeah. But it doesn't work.
She: What do you mean, it doesn't work?
He: See that there water trough?
She: Yes.
He: Well, the water is supposed to flow along
         there by gravity. But the principle of
         gravity just doesn't work.
She: Well, of course it doesn't work. You're
         trying to get gravity to make the water
         run uphill!

Odd, perhaps, but a way to illustrate the point that a principle is no less a principle just because it is misapplied. The principles governing human interaction are no different. Apply them correctly and they will work *for* you. Apply them incorrectly and they will work *against* you. Ignore them and you may never know why things didn't turn out the way you expected. So let's consider the correct and incorrect ways of applying these principles that influence attitude toward learning.

Conditions

Whenever students are in the presence of the subject they are learning, they are also in the presence of conditions. There is temperature, which may be too cold or too hot, and there is furniture, which may be too hard or too soft. Furthermore, there is the psychological environment, which may be hostile and tense or pleasant and supportive.

When naturally unpleasant conditions are paired with a subject being learned—that is, when they are present at the same time—the thing being learned can eventually come to evoke avoidance responses. That is, if a subject that initially has no special significance is presented to someone on several occasions while he or she is experiencing an aversive (unpleasant) condition, that subject may become a signal that triggers an avoidance response. Similarly, if a person is presented with a neutral subject and at the same time is in the presence of positive (pleasant) conditions, that subject may become a signal for an approach response.

Let's examine some everyday examples.

How do you react when a physician moves a hypodermic needle toward your arm? If you are like many people, you tend to back away; if you don't back away physically, you may turn your head to avoid seeing this signal for a forthcoming prick. There is nothing aversive about the sight of the hypodermic needle—the first time you see one, that is. The needle is a neutral object. But after you have experienced pain while in the presence of a hypodermic needle, the sight of the needle itself becomes a signal for an avoidance response.

I came across this magnificent example in a letter that appeared in an Ann Landers column:

> . . . When my mother took me shopping, I soon learned not to express an opinion. My taste was "atrocious." Hers was "elegant." Once when I saw a dress I really wanted, my mother said, in the presence of the saleswoman, "You are as fat as a pig and that dress makes you look like a freak."
>
> From then on I flatly refused to shop for clothes. I told my mother to bring home whatever she liked and I would wear it. I am a grown woman now, but these horrible memories are as vivid as if they had happened yesterday.
>
> I hate clothes and I wear my dresses till they fall apart. *To this day, I cannot pass the dress section where we used to shop without being physically ill* (italics added).*

Yes, neutral objects often turn into those that will attract or repel, and you will find many examples of them if you look. You may not find many that result in the extreme reaction cited above, but they are there nonetheless.

Going back to the study described in Chapter 5, there were several instances where the interviewees responded like this:

> "At first I didn't care much about the subject one way or the other. But the instructor made me feel very

* "Ann Landers" reprinted by permission of San Jose *Mercury* and Publishers-Hall Syndicate.

comfortable, and I began to worry less about a grade and found myself studying the subject more intently than I had planned."

And like this:

"I didn't know what to expect when I first started in the course. But all the instructors were so cheerful that I soon found myself looking forward to learning more about it."

NOTE: Affect feeling is unlike skill in at least two ways. First, nobody has to teach us to have affect. From birth, we all have all the skills needed to express the full range of emotions, both positive and negative. Second, unlike skills, an affect can switch polarity in the blink of an eye— either way. Events can turn a favorable attitude unfavorable, or cause a dislike of something or someone to take a turn toward the positive, in what seems like an instant. A colleague of mine tells this story:

"In college I had put my foot down against Wagner because all the guys were gaga over his music. Finally I *had* to take a required course in Wagner (ugh). I sat there for a couple of weeks, resisting for all I was worth, and then the instructor played a piece of music that changed everything. All of a sudden, like sand castles melting in the surf, my resistance crumbled, and in the space of a minute or so, my attitude changed 180 degrees."

We see, then, that one way of ensuring that we are not the cause of an avoidance tendency toward the subject matter we teach is to arrange our instructional environment so that students who are in the presence of the subject matter are, at the same time, (1) in the presence of positive conditions and (2) in the presence of as few aversive conditions as possible.

BUT. (There always seems to be a but in the ointment.) There is something else you must do to make this principle work for you. What?

You need to make sure that the conditions are considered favorable or pleasant by the students you are instructing. Like trying to make water run uphill, the principle won't work if it is misapplied; that is, if *you* are the only one who considers conditions positive.

The rule, then, is this:

> **When in the presence of the subject you are teaching, students should at the same time be in the presence of conditions *they* consider positive or favorable and in the presence of the fewest possible conditions *they* consider negative or unpleasant.**

A Common Misconception. Does application of this principle mean that instruction must be made "fun" and that students should not be required to work hard?

Not at all! Being in the presence of "work" is not necessarily the same as being in the presence of unpleasant conditions. Consider this dialogue:

"What kind of work do you do?"

"I'm in the sex business."

"The *what?*"

"The sex business. I teach actresses how to kiss."

"And you call that *work?*"

"It's not work, but it's a living."

This may seem an unlikely conversation, but it does serve to illustrate some of the confusion surrounding the word "work." This word has come to have several meanings. Sometimes it is used to refer to an occupation or profession, as in "What kind of work do you do?" When used this way, it seldom carries with it connotations of good or bad, pleasant or unpleasant. But *work* is also often used to refer to an activity that one would prefer to avoid, as in "Oh, that's work," or "I'd rather be enjoying myself, but I've got *work* to do." In these cases, the implication is that the activity referred to is one the speaker finds distasteful.

There is another way in which *work* is given a bad name. The familiar expression, "All work and no play makes Jack a dull boy," clearly implies that *play* is fun and *work* is not. What a horrible fate for a perfectly respectable word.

Were you to check your dictionary, you would find that *work* is "the expenditure of energy directed toward the accomplishment of something." It is engaging in some sort of purposeful activity. Skiing is work, swimming is work, playing the banjo is work, and so is writing. Haven't you ever engaged in purposeful activity that was exciting, engrossing, exhilarating, or just plain enjoyable? Haven't you ever heard anyone say, "I like my work"? Don't you like your work?

There must be something other than the expenditure of energy that causes the word "work" to have an aversive connotation with some activities and not with others. That something is the *conditions* associated with the activity or the *consequences* that follow the activity.

When energy expenditure is associated with aversive conditions, that activity will tend to become aversive; when the energy expenditure is followed regularly by aversive consequences (e.g., punishment), that activity will tend to be avoided.

There is nothing wrong with making students work. There is nothing wrong with making them work hard. But *there are a lot of things you can do to them while they are working* (while they are in the presence of the subject you are teaching) that can make the learning more, or less, attractive.

By all means make assignments, and by all means expect them to be carried out on time. But also do your best to see that these activities are associated with positive conditions and with as few aversive conditions as possible. After all, even under the best of circumstances you will not cause everyone to be wild about your favorite subject. But professional practice demands that you do everything in your power to make certain you don't accidentally destroy whatever interest is already there. *Don't confuse work with unpleasantness.*

Killing Success

There is something even worse than associating neutral subjects (those about which students don't care much one way or another) with unpleasant conditions, and that is to associate *favored* activities or subjects with unpleasant conditions. You'll recognize how this works when you read the following examples:

"All right! Just for that you can practice your piano for an extra hour!"

"OK. For that misbehavior, I'm going to give you twice as many math problems for homework!"

In other words, when an activity (such as studying or practicing) or a subject the student *likes* is used as a form of punishment, that activity may become less of a favorite activity. The rule is: NEVER to use as punishment an activity you would like your students to learn to love.

Consequences

Imagine yourself a student again. When you correctly answer a question posed by your instructor, the instructor smiles and says something like "Good." When you answer a question incorrectly, the instructor makes a comment such as, "Well, let's look at the question again." Wouldn't the probability increase that you will be willing to answer questions and come into contact with the subject matter? In any case, this kind of interaction would not adversely influence your responses toward the subject. Conversely, suppose each time you answer a question incorrectly, the instructor says, "Well, I see old Dumbo is at it again." How long do you think it would be before you stopped raising your hand? How long do you think it would be before you began to think of excuses for not attending class?

When experience with a subject is *followed* by a positive (pleasant) consequence, the probability is increased that the subject will be approached again in the future. When, on the other hand, experience with a subject is followed by aversive (unpleasant) consequences, the probability is reduced that the subject will be approached in the future.

Consider this scene, taken from a practice film intended to help people learn to apply these principles:[1]

Worker:	Hey, boss! I've got the problem solved, and the production run will cost at least 30 per cent less than we estimated.
Boss:	John, how many times do I have to ask you not to interrupt me while I'm working on budgets? . . . And will you please get that grubby apron cleaned?

[1] *Who Did What to Whom II?*, a film produced by Mager Associates (Carefree, AZ, 1982).

As you can well imagine, the worker's shoulders sag as he walks out of the scene. Wouldn't yours? After this scene is shown, the following questions are asked. You might try to answer them yourself; then compare your responses with mine.

1. What happened to the worker who solved the problem? (Be careful here. The question asks you to describe the event, rather than to make an interpretation of the event.)

2. Will the worker be more, or less, likely to report his successes to the boss in the future?

3. How could the boss have handled the situation more successfully? (That is, what could the boss have said or done to have caused consequences considered positive by the worker?)

Check your responses on the next page.

1. He was criticized for interrupting and criticized for his appearance.

2. Less likely. His performance led to humiliation.

3. The boss could have:

   - said something nice about the solution.
   - paid attention to the worker's description of a successful experience.
   - asked questions about the solution (another way of rewarding with attention).
   - whooped and hollered with joy.
   - called others and told them the good news.

Can you add five more possibilities?

Though this film example dealt with the workplace, the same principles hold in the classroom. Consider this scene. A student walks into an instructor's office, and this interchange follows:

> *Stud:*   I turned in my extra project a week ago. That was the report that took 40 hours of library research and writing. I was wondering if you've had a chance yet to review it.

> *Inst:*   (Rummaging through a pile of papers on the desk.) Have you seen my calendar? (More rummaging.) I just don't understand why someone would take my calendar and not bring it back.

> *Stud:*   (Walks out of the office, head hanging low.)

Answer these questions about the interchange.

1. What happened to the student who asked for feedback? (Again, the question asks for events rather than for interpretation of the events.)

2. Did the student consider the events to be favorable or unfavorable?

3. How do you know?

4. Will the student be more or less likely to work that hard on a report in the future?

5. How might the instructor have handled the interaction more appropriately?

Turn the page to check your responses.

1. The student was ignored. The instructor spoke of things other than the report being asked about.

2. Unfavorable.

3. The student walked out of the office (avoidance response) with head hung low.

4. Less likely. Actions followed by unpleasantness are less likely to be repeated.

5. The instructor could have:

    *   paid attention to the student.
    *   said something favorable about the student's report.
    *   asked questions about how the report was prepared.
    *   smiled.
    *   said something nice about the effort.

Can you add a few more possibilities?

Positive consequences, then, make it more likely that students will become favorably disposed toward your subject, and negative or unpleasant (aversive) consequences will make it less likely.

But again we have a but. But there are two things you have to do to make the principle work for you. First, you have to *follow* the behavior with the consequence; the favorable consequence must come *after* the desired performance.

The second thing you have to do to make the principle work for you is similar to what you have to do for conditions—make sure that the consequences are considered favorable by *the students*. It isn't good enough that *you* get pleasure from the consequences; the students must also experience them as positive or desirable. "You did such a good job on that lesson that I'm going to tell you all about how I got started in this field" may provide you with a great deal of satisfaction, but what about the students? Do they care? Or would they consider your story to be an event to endure?

The rule for consequences, then, is this:

Follow subject-matter contact with one or more consequences considered to be favorable by the students themselves.

This doesn't mean that you are expected to say or do something positive *each* and *every time* the students study or practice something. What it does mean is that the consequences should be positive rather than negative and that contact with the subject should lead to the students' worlds getting somewhat brighter rather than somewhat dimmer.

Accentuate the positive and eliminate the negative.

Once again, the correct application of this principle does not imply that you refrain from making your students work hard. It *does* mean that the hard work should be followed by a ray of sunshine rather than by a bonk on the head.

On to Specifics

The third way to increase the likelihood that you will send students away with a favorable attitude toward your subject is to model the performances you expect from your students. We'll consider modeling in Chapter 8.

Right now, let's think about exactly which conditions and events are positive and which are aversive.

Reprinted with special permission of King Features Syndicate.

7
Positives and Aversives

People learn to avoid the things
they're hit with.

Although it isn't always possible to know whether an event is positive or aversive for a given individual, some conditions and consequences are universal enough in their effect to provide considerable guidance. In this chapter we will examine some specific examples of positive and aversive conditions and consequences. Remembering that we're concerned with what is positive or aversive from the *students'* points of view, we'll begin with the negative. (That way we can end the chapter on a positive note.)

Aversives

An aversive condition or consequence is any event that causes physical or mental discomfort. It is any event that causes people to think less highly of themselves, that leads to a loss of self-respect or dignity, or that results in a strong anticipation of any of these. In general, any condition or consequence may be considered aversive if it causes a person to feel smaller or makes his or her world dimmer.

There are several conditions and consequences that are avoided by enough people to warrant their being referred to as *universal aversives.* When these conditions or consequences are associated with the subjects we teach, or appear as a result of subject matter contact, then the subject matter, learning, or even the learning environment itself may take on a less desirable hue . . . and no amount of righteous indignation on our part will alter this effect, and no declaiming of how the student "ought" to be more interested will have as much effect toward that end as reducing the aversive characteristics of the learning situation.

Pain

Pain is an acute physical discomfort, as you very well know. Though there are probably few situations left wherein instructors deliberately whop and bop their students, instructional pain is not yet extinct.

I know a violin instructor who, in an angry attempt to get his students' fingers properly positioned, makes those fingers hurt. He makes his students cry with pain and tremble with fear. His claim that this is "good" for the students is nothing more than justification for his uncommon version of educational malpractice.

Some people even believe that pain is good for students and good for learning. For example, you may have heard that idiotic expression, "If it ain't hard, it ain't learnin'." Meaning, "If it doesn't hurt, the instruction can't be any good."

We're talking here of pain inflicted by instructors as part of what they think to be "good instructional practice," rather than the kind of pain that may be an integral part of the subject matter. If you were learning to ride a horse, for example, you

DENNIS the MENACE

"HOW COME I DON'T HAVE A SPECIAL PLACE TO SIT WHEN I DO SOMETHIN' NICE?"

might experience a certain amount of pain in your . . . ah, well, backside. While that is a very real pain, it is horse-inflicted rather than instructor-inflicted. If you were learning to play football, you would experience a variety of kinds of pain that come from the game itself. If an instructor inflicts more pain than necessary to get the learning done, however, he or she is providing you with an example of primitive instructional practice.

When there *is* pain associated with learning the subject, instructors must go to greater pain (I just couldn't resist it) to counterbalance the aversives with positives. That is, instructors must try to make the learning experience net out as a positive one, by doing the kinds of things listed toward the end of this chapter.

Whether the pain is inflicted by the subject matter or by the instructor, pain is a condition people try to avoid. They do this either by learning to deal with the pain or by leaving.

Fear and Anxiety

Fear and anxiety are distress or uneasiness of the mind: apprehension of danger, misfortune, or pain; tension, stress, foreboding, worry, or disquiet; anticipation of the unpleasant.

Fear and anxiety are conditions that people try to avoid. When learning is associated with these states, the learner is more likely to learn to avoid the subject being taught.

Procedures leading to fear and anxiety are those that threaten various forms of unpleasantness. They include:

- Telling students by word or deed that nothing they can do will lead to success, or that contact with the subject will lead to undesirable consequences.
- Telling students, "You won't understand this, but . . ."
- Telling students, "It ought to be perfectly obvious that . . ."
- Threatening the exposure of "ignorance" by forcing individual students to solve problems in front of the class.

- Basing an attrition rate on administrative fiat rather than on student performance. ("Half of you won't be here a month from now," or "I don't believe in giving high grades.")
- Threatening failure by telling the student, "If you aren't motivated enough, you shouldn't be here." (Translation: "If you aren't motivated enough to learn in spite of my poor teaching, you certainly aren't going to get any help from me.")
- Being unpredictable about the standard of acceptable performance. (For example, a sixth-grade teacher told his students that they didn't have to listen to his discussion if they were having no difficulty with its topic. Five minutes later he berated half the class for "not paying attention.")
- Being unpredictable about the standard of acceptable performance (by telling students one thing and then testing them on something else).
- Letting it be known that the students' general behavior will be reported back to their bosses at the end of the course.
- Basing evaluations on performance unrelated to the skills being taught. ("Oh, sure, you learned it perfectly; but you seldom showed up on time, so I'm going to have to take ten points off for lateness." Or, "Oh, sure, you learned to do it perfectly; but you took more practice swings than most other students.")
- Letting visitors sit in the back of the room.
- Evaluating students by comparing one against the other, rather than by comparing each with the criteria of acceptable performance established in advance; e.g., "I grade on the curve."
- Suggesting that you will be reporting student progress to their supervisors.
- Creating stress unrelated to the learning, usually by making bizarre demands on classroom performance. ("Shine

your shoes"; "sit up straight"; "pick up your pencil"; "put down your pencil"; "stand up and recite the table of random numbers"; etc.)

Frustration

Frustration occurs when goal-directed activities are blocked, when purposeful or motivated activity is interfered with. To frustrate is to interfere with, to check, to make an effort come to no avail, to nullify, to defeat. Practices that can generate frustration include:

- Presenting information in larger units, or at a faster pace, than a student can assimilate. (The more motivated a student is, the greater the frustration when his or her efforts are blocked.) A colleague describes this as the situation where a student came to drink from the fountain of knowledge and somebody turned on a fire hose.*
- Speaking too softly to be heard easily (blocking students' efforts to come into contact with the subject).
- Keeping secret the intent of the instruction or the way in which performance will be evaluated.
- Providing unreadable print, type too small or too ornate, or vocabulary level too high.
- Providing obscure text, or implying more profundity than actually exists, as in, "When two parallel lines are cut by a transversal, the alternate interior angles are equal."
- Teaching one set of skills, and then testing for another.
- Testing for skills other than those stated in announced objectives.
- Refusing to answer students' questions.
- Forcing all students to proceed at the same pace, thus frustrating the slow and boring the quick.

* Courtesy of Jack Vaughn.

- Calling a halt when a student is absorbed with the subject or attempting to complete a project (ringing a school bell, for example).
- Returning work to a student after an unusually long period (several hours or more), thereby preventing the student from obtaining timely feedback on efforts expended.

Humiliation and Embarrassment

Humiliation and embarrassment are caused by lowering an individual's pride or self-respect by making someone uncomfortably self-conscious; by shaming, debasing, or degrading; or by causing a painful loss of dignity. Procedures that lead to these conditions include:

- Publicly comparing a student unfavorably with others.
- Laughing at a student's efforts. When a colleague returned his comments on the original draft of this book, he included the following:

  My own pappy relates his music career thusly: "We had a singing session and the teacher asked me to sing alone. When I did, all the kids laughed. The next day he asked me to do it again. Well, sir, I wouldn't do it. So the teacher made me come to the front of the class, but I still wouldn't do it. So he hit my hand with a ruler. But he could have cut off my fingers and I still wouldn't have done it. I didn't, either. Ever!"*

Another colleague penned the following:

  My creative writing professor at _____ asked if he could read a poem of mine to the class. I was flattered

* Courtesy of Dr. David Cram

until he proceeded to laugh at it, and provided oratory emphasis to emphasize his point. I got a "B" and stopped writing poetry shortly thereafter.*

- Spotlighting a student's weaknesses by bringing them to the attention of the class.
- Making a student wear a badge of his or her "stupidity" (putting him or her in a special seat or section or class, for example, or by requiring the student to keep the "dummy cup" on his or her desk until someone else "earns" the right to the same humiliation).
- Belittling a student's attempt to approach the subject by replying to his or her questions with answers such as "Stop trying to show off," or "Don't try to get ahead of the class."
- Insulting a student for his or her attempt to approach the subject by comments such as "You couldn't possibly understand the answer to that question," or otherwise telling the student by word or deed that his or her questions are considered stupid.
- Repeated failure. It is perfectly appropriate to challenge students enough to cause them to fail on occasion, provided that the *consequence* of failure isn't made deliberately aversive. Repeated failure, however, is sure to lead students to think less highly of themselves and to try to avoid the situations that have come to signify such a shrinkage of self-esteem.

Repeated failure is often engineered into our educational system. One practice is that of grading on a curve. Whenever a performance is evaluated by comparing it with how a number of chance neighbors happen to perform, students with the below-average aptitudes will almost always come out on the lower half of the curve.

* Courtesy of Verne Niner

They might have achieved all the objectives set out for them; they might have learned to work faster or more effectively; they may be exceeding the standard set out by the instructor. No matter. When their performances are compared with those of more talented neighbors, they will always be the losers. This use of the curve is only slightly less reprehensible than the instructor who brags that he or she has a "tough" course because 40 percent of the class "failed." (Has it ever occurred to the braggart that he or she is only 60 percent successful?)

• A common school practice leading to humiliation and embarrassment frequently occurs after a teacher has asked the class a question. In almost every class there seems to be at least one student who is so anxious to come into contact with the subject, so eager to demonstrate competence, that while frantically hand-waving for attention, he or she lets the answer slip out aloud. What is the consequence of this behavior? Does the student's world become a little brighter? Is he or she encouraged to think more highly of himself or herself as a result of this action? Sometimes. Often, however, the consequence is a finger pointed sternly in the student's direction, followed by, "I . . . didn't . . . call . . . on . . . you!" And what the student is learning is that it doesn't pay to get very excited about the things that happen in school, that showing too much interest can have unpleasant results, and that showing excitement can lead to embarrassment, to humiliation. Oh, I know. Students must be taught discipline (and discipline *will* be a problem as long as students are forced to sit in neat little rows listening to lectures). But there are better ways of handling discipline problems, ways that do not embarrass the student while in the presence of the subject matter.

Boredom

Boredom is caused by a situation in which the stimuli impinging on the student are weak, repetitive, or infrequent. Typical avoidance responses are those of leaving the situation and of falling asleep. Procedures leading to boredom include:

- Preventing students from taking an active role in their learning.
- Presenting information in a monotone.
- Rocking rhythmically back and forth while speaking.
- Insisting a student sit through instruction covering something that he or she already knows.
- Using impersonal, passive language.
- Providing information in increments so small that they provide no challenge or require no effort.
- Allowing lethargy-inducing temperatures to exist.
- Using only a single mode of presentation (no variety).
- Pairing students of considerably differing abilities, causing boredom to the faster and frustration and/or embarrassment to the slower.
- Reading the textbook aloud. Consider for a moment the effect on a student of the instructor whose principal technique is to read aloud from the textbook. If a student has prepared for the class by studying the assignment in the textbook, he or she is punished for this effort by having to listen to the same material during class. How can the student avoid some of the boredom? Very simply; by not doing his or her textbook assignments before coming to class. In this way, although the student may suffer through a dull reading of the textbook during the class hour, at least the material read will not be familiar. This is one situation where the student is rewarded for being less, rather than more, diligent. He or she is reinforced for disregarding the assignments of the instructor. Since this situation

is one in which the student's act of entering the classroom is followed by an unpleasant event (boredom), and since people tend to avoid unpleasant events, the student will simply try to avoid attending class whenever possible. And why not? Are *you* eager to place yourself in a boring situation? (Wake up there!)

- Going over material in class that was assigned as pre-reading. Similar to reading the text aloud, this practice promotes boredom. If students do, in fact, follow the instruction to read or study something before attending a class, they are almost certain to be bored during the early portion of the class. This is because most instructors cater to those who may *not* have followed the instructions regarding pre-reading. They go over the material regardless of whether students need it, thereby creating boredom for those who did as they were told. (In other words, following the directions is punishing. Students quickly learn that this can be avoided by not doing the pre-class assignment.)

Physical Discomfort

Physical discomfort is an uneasiness, a hardship, mild pain. Though there are several ways of inducing physical discomfort while the student is in the presence of a subject, many of them are not under the direct control of the instructor. A partial list of those within the instructor's control include:

- Allowing excessive noise or other distractions, such as calling students from the classroom to put out "brush fires" back at the office, allowing students to be interrupted by telephone calls, or requiring students to sit through "guest lectures" unrelated to the purpose of the course.
- Preventing students from moving around at will and from taking care of their personal needs (bathroom, toothache, headache, etc.).

- Requiring left-handed students to sit in those desk chairs that were obviously invented by a right-handed devil.
- Insisting that students be physically passive for longer periods of time than they can tolerate. Here is an example of how discomfort, combined with a reward, led to a most unexpected result:

> A woman had a ten-year-old son who attended Sunday school with some reluctance. She wanted him to feel more positive toward church. But the technique she selected for achieving this goal was to make the boy attend the *regular* service that followed the Sunday-school session. The boy found the regular service a very uncomfortable affair indeed. He had to sit in a hard pew . . . he had to be quiet . . . he had to restrain himself from fidgeting. In addition, he was expected to listen to something he didn't understand at all. Since "sitting in church" was aversive, it was rewarding to *leave* church, because church-leaving led to a turning off of the discomfort. Result: Church became a symbol of discomfort and boredom and was avoided whenever possible.

- Insisting that students pay close attention immediately after a meal.
- Making students travel farther between classrooms than can easily be accomplished in the time allotted.
- Making the classroom too hot or too cold.
- Requiring students to study under poor lighting conditions (such as is found in many hotel meeting rooms), leading to eyestrain and fatigue.

-
-

Using the Subject as Punishment

One school practice that produces aversive conditions and consequences is so common that I want to comment on it separately. This is the practice of using subject matter as an instrument of punishment. You know how it goes: "All right, because you were unruly, you can just stay after school and work 25 arithmetic problems," or "For that, you can just read four chapters tonight instead of the one chapter I was going to assign." Again, the issue has nothing to do with the appropriateness or inappropriateness of punishment. It concerns only the *instrument* of punishment. People tend to avoid the things they are hit with, whether it be a club, a stick, or a subject-matter assignment.

To keep herself from falling asleep while editing my manuscript, the editor will sometimes actually think about the subject she is reading. As she read the following paragraph, she was kind enough to offer the following example:

> "An instructor made an offender stay after class to do extra work, with a paper due at the end of the penalty session. Then, without looking at the paper, he tore it up in front of the student."

No doubt about it. When the subject matter itself is used as a form of punishment, students will quickly learn that the subject is something to be avoided.

So much for the negative side of the issue. Now let's consider the positive side, because that's where we'll find the golden practices through which we can improve attitude toward learning.

Positives

A *positive condition or consequence* is any pleasant event that exists during the time the student is in the presence of the subject matter or that follows his or her interaction with the subject matter. A positive condition or consequence causes the student to think a little more highly of himself or herself and causes the student's world to become a little brighter.

Conditions and consequences that are *universal positives* are just the opposite of the universal aversives. They are the events that lead to success experiences and then acknowledge that success, ensure a variety of stimulation, lead to an increase of self-esteem or improved self-image, and lead to an increase in confidence. Positive practices include:

- Acknowledging students' responses, whether correct or incorrect, as attempts to learn, and following them with accepting rather than rejecting comments ("Try doing it *this* way," rather than "How could anyone make such a stupid error!").
- Reinforcing or rewarding subject approach responses (by a smile, a favorable word, a cheer, a cup of coffee or a lunch, or a little attention).
- Sending a student or three to look at a particularly good piece of work completed by another student.
- Providing a tangible token for successful completion of a particularly difficult or time-consuming piece of work. (In one of our workshops we literally use a large gold sticker, suitably imprinted for the occasion. Though a few of our students—adults—make pooh-pooh comments about the "gold star," they make sure they don't leave without it.)
- Providing instruction in increments that will allow success most of the time.
- Eliciting learning responses in private rather than in public.
- Providing enough signposts so that students always know where they are and where they're expected to go.

- Providing students with statements of instructional objectives that they can understand when they first see them.
- Detecting what individual students already know, and then adjusting the curriculum in order to avoid boring individuals by teaching them what they already know.
- Providing feedback that is immediate and specific to a student's response.
- Giving students some choice in selecting and sequencing of the subject matter (especially if the insructor maintains rigid control over the goals of the instruction), thus making positive involvement possible.
- Providing students with some control over the length of the instructional session.
- Relating new information to old, within the experience of each student.
- Treating students as individuals, rather than as numbers in a faceless mass.
- Using active rather than passive words during presentations.
- Pointing to student progress by comparing today's performance to yesterday's performance (e.g., "You completed twice as many modules today."), rather than by comparing today's performance to perfection (e.g., "You've still got a long way to go before you sing like Pavarotti.").
- For managers only: Allowing only those instructors who like and are enthusiastic about their subjects (and students) to teach.
- Making sure students can perform with ease, not just barely, so that confidence can be developed.
- Expressing genuine delight at seeing each student ("*Delighted* to see you again!").
- Expressing genuine delight at seeing a student succeed.
- Providing instructional tasks that are relevant to the objectives.

- Using only those test items relevant to the objectives.
- Allowing students to move about as freely as their physiology and their curiosity demand.

Positive Practices

In the study described in Chapter 5, interviewees made the following comments about teacher practices that had a positive influence on their interest in the subject under discussion:

"He taught us how to approach a problem so we could solve it for ourselves. He gave us the tools for learning."

"He broke down the subject matter into pieces we could understand. When we couldn't understand something, he tried to find another way of approaching it."

"She made books available at our level. That is, these were books that answered questions we had about the subject at that particular time."

"The instructor reinforced our desire to learn by giving us assistance and by showing a personal interest in what we were doing."

"He led discussions but did not dominate them."

"She had a magnificent manner of presentation; she taught history as though it were a news-analysis course, tying current happenings to historical happenings."

"He was always able to make individual students understand what was expected of them and where they stood."

"She used a lot of variety; she brought in other instructors, used videos and demonstrations rather than pure lecture."

"He asked, and respected, the opinion of students ... even though he didn't always agree with them."

"She knew her subject and always appeared to have time to help me."

There is nothing revolutionary about the procedures listed in this chapter. Every instructor interested in increasing the capabilities of his or her students uses many or all of them, and others as well.

Then why go into such detail? Simply because *good intentions are not enough*. Though we are generally in favor of sending students away at least as interested in our subject as they were when they arrived, we do little or nothing to *ensure* that this is the case. Such apathy is frightening if one considers that the continuing use of tactics leading to subject avoidance represents an enormous loss of potential skills. Those lost skills may well be one of the greatest burdens our economy will have to carry as we move into an age where a person without economic and social skills will be virtually unemployable.

8
Modeling

People see, people do.

Me: If it is your desire that when instructing, your students confine themselves to an expository style of least complexity consistent with the subject matter and the target population, such an outcome is more probable of accomplishment if your own exposition is isomorphic to that which is desired.

You: Huh?

Me: If you want your students to use plain language when they teach, you should use plain language when you teach.

You: Why didn't you say so?

Me: I just did.

You: Then how come you don't use simple language when you teach?

Me: Don't do as I do, do as I say!

That silly little dialogue should serve to illustrate the essence of the modeling principles, which is—practice what you preach.

While it's true that we learn by practicing, by doing, and by being rewarded for our progress, it is also true that most of what we learn is learned by imitation. Most of what we learn comes from watching others do things that we then try to do—and then become able to do. When we see others do something, there is a tendency for us to imitate their actions. People see, people do.

This means that attitude toward (or away from) learning is strongly influenced by modeling. How does it work?

Modeling influences people mainly by informing them of a way of doing something. When something is demonstrated by a model, the observer sees, or hears of, a way in which that thing can be done. It may not be the right way or the desired way or the safe way, but the way shown is likely to be the way that is adopted.

Suppose you are vacationing overseas and a family asks you to have dinner. As you sit down to the meal, you notice unfamiliar utensils alongside your plate. Since you don't know what they are for, what should you do? One appropriate way to react would be to ask what the utensils are for and how they are used. But it's more likely that you would watch what your host and hostess did and then follow suit, imitating the behavior that they modeled.

Fair enough. But how does this apply to a course? Well, have you ever had a course in which the instructor made unfavorable comments about the subject he or she was teaching?

"This is a required course, and I don't like it any better than you do."

"I don't know why I was assigned to teach this course, but I suppose we'd better get on with it."

"This is terribly uninteresting, but ..."

"This is a dull video, but I'm supposed to show it."

After reading these comments, a colleague reviewing this manuscript said, "I jumped at the chance to take a course in general semantics from Hayakawa himself. His teaching assistant actually said to me, 'Anybody stupid enough to take this course should get an automatic F.'"

It isn't easy to maintain one's enthusiasm in the face of comments like these. And have you ever attended a course in which the instructor just went through the motions of teaching—never smiled or said anything favorable about the subject being taught, simply recited old notes, and seemed as glad to leave the room as you were? Again, it's hard to maintain a favorable attitude toward anything when apathy is what is being modeled.

Would you know how to hold a knife if you wanted to kill someone? Sure you would. You've seen it modeled on television. Would you know where to kick a man to put him out of business? Sure you would. You've seen that modeled on television, too. Hundreds of times. You've seen a lot of things modeled there, things you now know how to do even though you will never do them. Why do you suppose influence groups try to stop programs from being shown on television? In part, it's because they don't want us to have certain attitudes and skills modeled for us, because they don't want us to see how *others* behave toward one thing or another. They know that television is a powerful modeling medium and that modeling changes behavior. (It's interesting that, on the one hand, the TV people try to convince us that television—and the sex and violence depicted there—*doesn't* influence people; on the other hand, TV people try to sell advertising by convincing their clients that TV *does* influence people.)

Modeling Principles

There are several principles of modeling. The more important ones are listed here, along with an example or two to show you how each principle may be applied to the instructional environment.

1. **Observers learn by watching and imitating others; they tend to behave as they have seen others behave.**

   Application Example. Behave in the classroom the way you want others to behave. If you want students to observe certain safety precautions when handling equipment, then *you* observe those safety precautions. If you want students to do what you tell them to do (whether you do the telling in person or through your writing or other medium of communication), make sure there is no discrepancy between what you tell and what you do.

How *strongly* an observer will tend to imitate modeled performance is influenced by several factors. The following principles describe some of them.

2. **Observers will be more likely to imitate a model who has prestige in the eyes of the observers.**

   Application Example. Have desired performance demonstrated by someone your students respect: a manager, local hero, football player, or movie star. (You can imagine the delight experienced by the students when the teacher invited a local football hero to help her read Shakespeare to the class.) And don't forget that instructors often have prestige in the eyes of students, so it is doubly important that you practice what you preach.

3. **Observers will be more likely to imitate modeled performance when they observe the model being reinforced for that performance.**

   Application Example. Arrange to have a demonstrator of desired performance (the model) applauded, awarded a trophy, given a raise, or praised—in the presence of the observers.

Application Example. A workshop participant offered this personal experience: "My own reports were always very descriptive (also long) until one day I heard my boss being congratulated for being concise in writing a one-page, fully satisfactory report. I now make it a point to be concise, too."

4. **Observers who see a model being punished will tend not to imitate the performance that was punished.**

Application Example. When someone is demonstrating correct performance, be sure he or she is not accidentally punished in the presence of observers. Also, when participants do something wrong, be sure they are corrected; be sure they don't "get away" with it. (If the chief instructor cannot get away with parking in the president's parking place, the students will be less likely to try it.)

Application Example. (Also from a previous workshop participant.) "A colleague was told by our boss that he was too busy to see him. I have since had a tendency to wait until he calls me rather than try to make an appointment to see him. Ever since my colleague was 'put down' when trying to see the boss, I have tried to see him only on matters of utmost urgency."[1]

The research on modeling tells us that *if we would maximize subject-matter approach tendencies in our students, we must exhibit those behaviors ourselves.* In other words, we must behave the way we want our students to behave.

[1] Examples and other material in this chapter are taken from *CRI (Criterion-Referenced Instruction): Practical Skills for Designing Instruction that Works,* Fourth Edition; by R.F. Mager and Peter Pipe (Center for Effective Performance, Atlanta, GA, 1994).

Although a display of interest and enthusiasm is not enough to guarantee that students will come to display similar feelings, the probability is certainly greater that this will happen than if we display apathy and loss of interest. Conversely, a display of apathy on our part doesn't prevent a student from becoming more interested in our topics . . . but it doesn't help. Research confirmed years ago that when you teach one thing and model something else, the teaching is less effective than if you practice what you teach. The father, for example, whose approach is to say, "Stop fighting with the other kids or I'll whip you good," is less likely to be successful than if he were to model the kind of behavior he is interested in teaching. Parents are less likely to teach their kids to love their neighbor when the parents continually fight among themselves than if they were to model the behavior they want to teach. And, as Dr. Albert Bandura suggests, the father who exhorts his children to work hard in school, while he guzzles beer in front of the TV, is less likely to see the desired behavior than if he were to model the beaver instead of the sloth.[2]

What students learn by imitation, however, is not confined to their attitudes relating to various academic topics. For example, one professor who teaches psychology spends a great deal of time teaching students how to read and interpret journal articles. He teaches them how to recognize the difference between data and the interpretation of data and how to recognize the difference between adequate and inadequate controls. At the same time, he is also modeling a certain kind of behavior with regard to criticism. When a student condemns a research report because of a design flaw, this instructor says, "Perhaps. But what is the author trying to say? What is good about the study?" When a student is hypercritical because of the way in which a report is written, the instructor asks, "How could the author have said it better?" In other words, rather

---

[2] *Social Foundations of Thought and Action*, by Albert Bandura (Prentice-Hall, 1986); see Chapter 2.

than model nit picking criticism, this instructor models positive criticism, and it is likely his students will learn to do the same. If we would like to increase the frequency with which our students think critically or open-mindedly, we have a better chance of succeeding if we demonstrate these qualities ourselves. If we would have our students demonstrate a love for learning, we have a better chance of succeeding if we demonstrate that a quest for knowledge is more important than simply parroting what is in the text.

Are We Models Worthy of Imitation?

There's an easy way to find out. All you have to do is record one or two of your instructional sessions on videotape and then observe the results. (If you manage to sit through the entire playback without falling asleep, you can tell yourself you aren't too bad.) As you watch the playback, ask yourself these questions. Did you:

- spend time looking at the people you were talking to?
- use variety in your voice inflection (i.e., avoid monotone)?
- smile when you talked, at least part of the time? (Do a "smile count." If you don't smile at least once every five minutes, you need some practice there.)
- say something positive about what you were teaching?
- say why others should find the topic of interest?
- refrain from hypnotic movements, such as swaying back and forth?
- refrain from negative comments, such as "This is sort of dull, but . . ."?
- refrain from demeaning or insulting students when they displayed interest in the subject?
- when showing or demonstrating, do it the way you want your students to do it?

NOTE: There are other procedures that are more or less effective in influencing behavior, but a thorough discussion of each is beyond the scope of this book. I will only mention that exhortation, a procedure used regularly for centuries, has seldom been very successful in influencing behavior (e.g., "Pay close attention now, because in several weeks this material will become very important!"). The instructor who does little more than insist his or her students be interested, or insist they be motivated, will certainly have cause for complaining about student apathy.

There are some other things you can do to find out how successful you are in influencing attitude toward learning, and these will be considered in the next chapter.

Where We Are

We have considered three important means by which attitude toward learning, and toward the subject being taught, may be influenced:

- conditions that exist during the learning,
- consequences that occur as a result of trying to learn, and
- modeling of desired performance.

But there's more. Until now we've been concerned with ways to influence attitudes in a favorable way. Now it's time to learn how to make sure your students will be willing to *use* what you have taught them. It's time to learn about the concept of *self-efficacy*.

9
Self-Efficacy

Now you're ready for the big leagues.

You're ready to learn about a powerful technique for influencing whether your students will be willing to use the skills you've taught them and whether they will be able to persevere in the face of periodic failures or other kinds of adverse circumstances. In other words, you'll learn how to help your students turn their favorable attitudes into energetic action. You'll learn how to strengthen their *self-efficacy*. Let me begin with a story or three to set the stage.

The debater. Charlie hadn't even known there was such a thing as a debating course before signing up, but he thought he'd give it a try. He found that he enjoyed the experience. During the course, he enjoyed researching his assigned debate topics and did a good job in presenting his arguments. Even the instructor commented favorably on how his presentations were received.

Soon after the course ended, he was invited to join the varsity debating team. But he declined. He hung back, and no amount of encouragement caused him to change his mind. He just didn't believe his skill was as good as he was told it was.

The scientist. Sharon was a research scientist. She had published several papers in respected journals and was often invited to present papers at professional meetings. She liked her work and was good at what she did. Soon she came to the attention of a prestigious laboratory, which offered her a position of a life-time: her own lab, lab assistants, a good budget to work with—and all this in a location she liked.

But she turned it down. Why? Her explanation was, "I didn't think I was good enough. I didn't think I could live up to their expectations."

The math student. Some years ago I conducted a learning experiment in a boys' school in Italy. During lunch one day, one of the instructors told me a story about one of his boys. It seems that this boy, who was good at math, took a math test one day, and in answer to the question, "How much is ten divided by one?" wrote *eight*. When asked how he arrived at that answer, the boy replied, "Well, I knew the answer was ten, but our teachers always tell us that when you divide, the answer *has* to be smaller than the number you started with. So I figured if ten wasn't right, the answer must be nine."

"But you wrote down *eight*," said the puzzled teacher. "Why was that?"

"Well," replied the boy, sheepishly, "everybody always tells me how stupid I am. So I figured if I put down the *right* answer, they would think I was cheating."

What do these three stories have in common? One liked debating, one liked science, and the third liked math. In each case, the person had a favorable attitude toward the subject described. But even a favorable attitude wasn't enough to give them the "courage of their convictions." The debater didn't believe he had the skill for the varsity debating team. The sci-entist didn't believe she was good enough to accept a "dream" job. And the math student didn't feel confident enough in his skill to write what he knew to be the right answer.

In each case, there was a favorable attitude toward the sub-ject; what was missing was that they didn't *believe* they had the skill that they actually had.

And that's how the concept of self-efficacy differs from the concept of attitude. While it is possible to have a favorable attitude toward a subject or activity, it is at the same time possible to believe that the subject-related skills are weaker or less developed than they actually are. And that causes people to hang back from something they would really like to do. It causes them not to persevere in the face of adverse circumstances.

What Is Self-Efficacy?

Self-efficacy refers to the *judgments* that people make about their abilities to execute particular courses of action—about their *ability to do specific things*. For example, "I know I can give a talk in front of large audiences," "I know I can sew a straight seam by hand," "I know darn well that I can sing this aria skillfully and without forgetting the lyrics."

Self-efficacy isn't about the actual skills that people have; it's about the *judgments* people make about what they can do with those skills. People with low self-efficacy don't believe that they can do the things they actually can do. On the other hand, people with high self-efficacy usually make more realistic judgments about what they can do. When their skills in an area are strong, they judge them to be strong and are willing to act on that judgment.

Why Is Self-Efficacy Important?

The importance of strong self-efficacy cannot be overestimated. Dr. Albert Bandura said it best in "Organizational Applications of Social Cognitive Theory," an article published in the December 1988 issue of the *Australian Journal of Management:*

"People who have a strong belief in their capabilities think, feel, and behave differently from those who have doubts about their capabilities. People who doubt their capabilities shy away from difficult tasks. They have low aspirations and weak commitment to the goals they choose to pursue. Failure wrecks their motivation . . . They give up quickly in the face of difficulties and are slow to recover their confidence following failure or setbacks."

Note that it is possible to have high self-efficacy about a specific performance and, at the same time, expect that it will produce negative results. For example, "I know I can make a terrific sales presentation, but I also know I won't get the contract." Self-efficacy refers to judgments about performing a specific act, rather than to expectations about the consequences or outcomes of that act.

Why Is Self-Efficacy Important to Instructors?

Because people with low self-efficacy are made, not born. Because the actions of instructors can make the difference between a willingness to *try* to apply what was learned and a tendency to quit. Because instructors can make their students less (or more) vulnerable to on-the-job conditions that aren't always supportive and can help them survive rejection and periodic failures.

How Is Self-Efficacy (SE) Strengthened?

There are five types of things you can do to strengthen SE:

1. Ensure performance mastery.

The most powerful way to strengthen SE regarding an ability to do something is to make sure students learn to do that thing well. But mastery is not enough, because mastery is just raw data. Unless students are also taught that the mastery is a result of their own efforts, they may leave you thinking things such as "The instructor helped me," or "I only did it right because of the job aid," or "Other students helped me," or "I was just lucky." For performance to have a maximum effect, students must learn that *they* are the cause of the performance. Here's how:

- Arrange for enough independent practice so that mastery, as defined by course objectives, is achieved or surpassed.
- Break the learning into manageable chunks that have definite end points. That will increase the number of successes that the students can experience.
- Cast your feedback comments in terms of progress achieved, rather than in terms of learning yet to be accomplished.

> *Right:* "Your work shows fewer spelling errors today than it did yesterday."
> *Wrong:* "You've got a long way to go before your spelling will be good enough."

2. Model desired performance.

You've already learned about the importance of modeling, so you need only to be reminded of how to make modeling work for you rather than against you.

- Ensure that you do it (i.e., demonstrate the skills) and talk about it the way you want your students to do it and talk about it.
- Use models (demonstrators) similar to the students, and make sure that the students understand that the modeled behavior is due to the skill of the model, rather than to other factors.
- Have the model make task-diagnostic comments during or after a performance (see task-diagnostic section below).

3. Use task-diagnostic feedback.

We can interpret feedback in either self-diagnostic or task-diagnostic ways, and the way we do it will have an enormous (often life-long) effect on self-efficacy. Here's what these two concepts mean:

Self-diagnostic feedback. When people have been made self-diagnostic, they interpret failure and negative feedback as personal deficiencies, as a reflection of their ability and on their potential to learn more. They may also blame others when they fail. For example, "They didn't give me enough time," or "The boss didn't explain it clearly."

Students develop the habit of thinking self-diagnostically when family or teachers make comments that imply personal deficiencies. Comments such as these, for example, can cause enormous harm:

"You'll never amount to much."

"You're not working up to your potential."

"You're just being forgetful again."

"How can you expect to learn this if you don't pay attention?"

"You just don't have the knack for this."

"You can do better than that."

"Oh, oh. Here comes Clumsy again."

"You could do it if you really tried."

"You'll have to wait till you're older."

Notice that not one of these feedback comments says anything whatever about the quality or accuracy of the performance giving rise to the comment. Not one offers information about how the performance might be improved. Instead, each comment suggests a personal deficiency, something "wrong" with the performer. Each one slaps a label of "not good enough" on the performer. Even worse, the last two comments provide an excuse for not even trying.

Task-diagnostic feedback. In contrast to self-diagnostic feedback, task-diagnostic feedback focuses on the task being performed. This type of feedback comments on characteristics of the performance itself, rather than the performer, and usually offers information about how the performance might be improved. Task-diagnostic feedback interprets failure as information, rather than as evidence of some sort of deficiency on the part of the learner. Examples:

> "If you hold your fingers together like this, it should go better next time."

> "If you use the job aid, it will help keep you from skipping any of the problem-solving steps."

> "This error happened because at this point you added, instead of subtracting."

> "This objective looks good, but you need to add a criterion of acceptable performance."

> "The session recording shows that you provided your students more practice time today than last week. Here's what I think you can do to increase the practice time to at least 50% of lesson time."

Notice that these task-diagnostic comments focus on the tasks rather than on the performers. It's comments such as these that will act to strengthen self-efficacy. Here's what to do in practice:

- Focus feedback comments on characteristics of the performance itself and on ways to improve the performance, rather than on student characteristics.

- Avoid deliberately making students fail in public. For students with low SE, public failure will be more destructive—not only to the performer, but to observers who also happen to be low on SE. For example, don't allow students to perform in front of an entire class until their skill and SE levels are high.

- Arrange for students to experience successes (e.g., mark the *right* answers rather than the wrong ones). Relate student performance to progress toward achievement of the objective.

- Help students interpret their "failures" as being not-yet-competent performance. (As they begin learning a new skill, they are *expected* to make mistakes. If someone labels each and every imperfect practice attempt as another failure, their SE will suffer.)

- Provide students with clear-cut, near-term goals.

- Once a skill has been mastered, provide practice under a range of conditions, so that students can judge themselves competent to handle the actual situations they are likely to encounter.

4. **Strengthen favorable attitude.**

Students who are favorably disposed toward the subject they are learning are more likely to develop subject-related skills. Because skill promotes high self-efficacy, instructors should focus on the development of a favorable attitude toward the target subject. That's what this book is mainly about, of course, so if you apply the techniques described herein, you will go a long way toward strengthening SE in your students. As a reminder:

- Arrange for students to perform successfully, and then be sure to help them interpret their achievements as evidence of increasing capability. For example, "You can see that as a result of your own efforts, you can do that faster (or better) than you'll ever be expected to do it on the job."

5. Interpret physiological information.

People tend to make inferences about their ability from physiological cues such as pain, effort, windedness, emotional arousal, etc. If something is difficult to do, they may very well conclude that they don't have the ability to do it. For example, because I find writing difficult, I've never thought of myself as a writer—even though the writing has proven successful. To me, "real writers" are people whose fingers fly as soon as they sit down at their keyboard (or quill pen), even though they keep telling me I'm wrong. In other words, I confuse the difficulty of writing with my ability to do it. (Having been made aware of the problem, I've managed to invent ways to solve it—for me.)

This is not an uncommon misconception, especially among young students whose self-efficacy may have been damaged at home (e.g., "Why can't you be as smart as your sister?"). Such unfortunates are likely to want to give up as soon as they discover that what they're trying to do requires work.

Your job is to help them understand that the *difficulty* of accomplishing is not necessarily related to their *ability* to accomplish. After all, lots of things require effort; learning to play golf or other sports, learning to play a musical instrument, becoming any kind of a skilled professional, and so on. If students are allowed to conclude that the difficulty of the task defines their ability to learn it, they will lose many opportunities to master what might become highly enjoyable and/or useful skills. What to do?

- Make sure that students do not interpret physiological cues that signify effort (i.e., cues that say, "Hey, there's some hard work going on here!") as a lack of ability.
- Model (demonstrate) finding pleasure in the hard work; e.g., aerobics class instructors who say, "Wow, this is tough," while laughing, smiling, and doing more.
- If experiencing pain, discomfort, or difficulty at a certain point in the learning is normal or a sign of progress (e.g., "no pain, no gain"), say so to the students.

It is critical that the judgments students make about their ability to perform specific tasks (self-efficacy) come close to matching the true level of their skills. With high SE, students will be more likely to try and to persevere in the face of obstacles and occasional failures. It's worth doing all you can to help your students achieve the exhilarating state of high self-efficacy.

And Now?

Now that you know how to develop favorable attitudes and strengthen self-efficacy, let's consider some ways to find out how well your efforts are paying off.

Self-Efficacy Checklist

When you want to find out whether your SE strengthening practices are on track, you may want to use the Self-Efficacy Checklist on the following page as a guide. It includes items specifically relating to improvement of self-efficacy and will help you spot opportunities for improvement.

An Attitude Checklist, included in Chapter 11, is a more comprehensive checklist that will provide reminders about which instructional practices to review when you plan a more complete checkup of your attitude-influencing methods and procedures.

SELF-EFFICACY CHECKLIST

A "YES" answer to the following questions assures that trainee self-efficacy will be strengthened. A "NO" answer represents an opportunity for improvement.

	YES	?	NO
1. Is each trainee allowed to practice until he/she can perform to the criteria stated in the objectives?			
2. Does the training arrange for *private* practice (to the degree consistent with the objectives) and feedback?			
3. Are the conditions under which the practice occurs as close to real world conditions as possible?			
4. Does the feedback remind trainees that their performance was due to their own skill rather than to other factors?			
5. Does the feedback focus on performance improvement, rather than on the aptitude of the trainee?			
6. Does the feedback describe gains (i.e., progress toward the objective) rather than shortfalls (i.e., learning yet to be accomplished)?			
7. Are trainees provided with proximal (near-term) goals toward which to work?			
8. After a skill has been mastered, is practice given under the range of conditions described by the objective?			
9. Are the demonstrations conducted by someone similar to the trainees in attributes (e.g., age, sex, status)?			
10. Does the model demonstrate the same job or performance that the trainees are expected to learn?			
11. Does the demonstrator make task-diagnostic comments during or after the demonstration?			
12. When cognitive strategies are being taught, does the model verbalize those strategies when demonstrating the skills to be learned?			
13. Have steps been taken to help trainees understand that high effort does not mean a lack of capability?			

Part III

How Will I Know I've Arrived?

10
Evaluating Results

"You can't measure the effects of what I do."
"Why not?"
"They're intangible."
"Oh? Why should I pay you for intangible results?"
"Because I've been trained and licensed to practice."
"Hmmm . . . all right. Here's your money."
"Where? I don't see it."
"Of course not . . . it's intangible!"

Can we talk? In this chapter we're going to consider how you might find out how well your efforts to improve student attitude and self-efficacy are paying off. Before we do, though, we need to put this business of self-review in perspective. It's easier than it may look.

First point. The business of "cleaning up our act" is an ongoing process. We don't apply a set of procedures intended to improve attitudes and then forget about it forever. Improving the effectiveness of our instruction and improving our success at sending students away with favorable attitudes toward the subject of the instruction are things we continue to think about—things we constantly make adjustments to.

Second point. Any self-assessment activity in which we choose to engage is private. Nobody has to see the results of our efforts at self-review. It's like climbing up on the bathroom scale; nobody has to know whether the scale is applauding, laughing its fool head off, or hollering "Help!"

Third point. Because you are looking for indications of progress toward your goal, and because the information you collect will be private, you can relax. Also, because you are looking for progress indicators, rather than looking for scientific data to publish in the *Psychological Journal of Superbly Wrinkled Attitudes,* you needn't be concerned about statistics or any other form of sophisticated mathematical gyrations. You just want to find out whether there are some rough spots in your instruction that you can smooth out and whether you're moving in the right direction. Period.

Since there is something to be learned from earlier attempts to measure so-called intangibles, we will begin here.

Where's Your Intelligence? For many years, there was a serious search for what might be called the single-measure test of intelligence. Scientists measured the length of the forehead or the number and location of bumps on the head and tried to correlate their measurements with something called *intelligence.* But it was all in vain.

For one thing, there is no such "thing" as intelligence in the sense that there is a heart and a brain. Intelligence is not a structure or an organ that can be measured with a pair of calipers or a scale. Intelligence consists of several capabilities or capacities that cannot be accurately predicted by any *single* physical measurement.

Another reason the attempt to find the single-measure test of intelligence failed is that intelligence is a multi-faceted characteristic that can only be inferred indirectly. That is to say, intelligence, like attitudes, is a characteristic that is inferred

Sometimes it's difficult to remember that the invention of a word, such as "intelligence," doesn't guarantee that there is a descriptive object to go with that word. I can invent a word like "bolguin," for example, or talk about "three-headed Martians," but that doesn't mean that bolguins and three-headed Martians really exist.

from circumstantial evidence. It is a form of prediction about how skillfully someone might handle a given situation, based on what that person has been seen to do.

If we want to measure intangible characteristics such as "intelligence," we must first decide what the concept means, and then we must collect information that will tell us whether someone does or does not have characteristics that conform to our meaning of the concept.

Like the trait "intelligence," "favorable attitude toward _____" is an invisible characteristic. If we want to find out whether students have a favorable attitude toward our subject, we need to collect some items of evidence that will indicate just what "favorable attitude toward _____" is in terms of the things we want students to do or say in relation to that subject.

How can we do that? There are two things we can do to collect information we need regarding student attitude and self-efficacy:

1. We can collect information about how students feel about the subject.

2. We can observe what students actually do as a result of contact with our subject.

Here's how.

How Do They Feel?

If I say to a student, "Hullo, there. How do you feel about my subject?" and get a response of "Phffft," I know that all is not well. On the other hand, if the response is "Gee, it's terrific!," I can be more optimistic. I would want more evidence than that one comment before concluding that this student has a favorable attitude toward the subject, but it's a start.

Similarly, if a student fell asleep in my class, I wouldn't immediately conclude that this behavior was the result of my instruction. After all, there are events not under my control that might lead to dozing off; a hard night before, getting up unusually early in the morning, drugs, illness, etc. (In our workshops, we actually encourage students to drop off for a bit if they feel the need. Since we don't lecture at them, they won't miss anything; and when they awake, they'll be refreshed and ready to pick up where they left off.)

Don't neglect direct questions. Sometimes the direct approach is quickest, least expensive, and most valid. Probably the best way for me to find out whether you like pistachio nuts is to come right out and ask you. If you say, "I like them very much," I have better evidence from which to infer an approach tendency than if I had not asked such a direct question. We can learn a lot about people simply by asking them direct questions.

An experiment was once described to me that bears on the importance of the direct question. The military was reported to have conducted an experiment to find out how they could predict which soldiers would perform well in arctic weather. They gave a large number of soldiers personality and aptitude tests, they measured blood pressure and other physiological variables, and they used questionnaires. After all the data were gathered, analyzed, and digested, they found that the best predictor of whether someone would function well in arctic weather was simply to ask, "Do you like cold weather?" If the reply was "Heck, no!", it was a sure bet that he or she wouldn't do well in the Arctic.

The Questionnaire

The answer to the "How do you feel?" question can be obtained with a questionnaire or by simply asking the student (privately) a question or two that will tell you what you want to know.

Though it would be possible (and scientifically acceptable) to administer a questionnaire at the beginning, as well as at the end, of the instruction, to measure attitude shifts, I don't recommend it. It's awkward, it's intrusive, and it's unnecessary. The last thing you want to do to students when they enter your course is to provide them with an obstacle that will delay their learning. "Good morning. Before we do anything else, I want you to answer the questions on this questionnaire. This will tell us how you feel about the subject of this course, so that we can compare that with your feelings at the end of the course." If they don't run for the exit, you will have at least frustrated their entry into the subject.

So, if you use a questionnaire, use it at the very end of the instruction, when it will be possible to convince the student that honest responses to the questionnaire won't have any influence on his/her grade. (We ask our students to complete a short evaluation form after the student has received his/her Certificate of Achievement. We also ask them during the course to tell us about obstacles and other practices that we can correct or improve on the spot.)

What kind of questions might you use? Consider using those that ask students:

- how they feel about the subject, and how they think they might behave when placed in certain situations or when asked certain questions.
- to make choices involving your subject.

Here are some examples of possibly useful items. As you read through them, remember that there are more sample questions than you will need; four or five of the more appropriate ones should be enough.

Sample Questionnaire Items

Since instructional environments differ in many ways, it is not possible to provide a complete questionnaire that will work in all situations. You will have to consider the items that follow as suggestions. Use the ones that apply, and derive your own from those that don't apply directly. Although the items are numbered consecutively, they are not listed in any order of importance.

1. Do you intend to take another course in _____?
   a. Yes.
   b. No.
   c. I'm not sure.

2. How interested are you in taking another course in _____?
   a. Very interested.
   b. Somewhat interested.
   c. I don't care one way or the other.
   d. Not too interested.
   e. Not at all interested.

3. How interested are you in learning more about _____?
   a. Very interested.
   b. Somewhat interested.
   c. I don't care one way or the other.
   d. Not too interested.
   e. Not at all interested.

4. If I had it to do all over again, I (would/would not) take this course.

5. I find the subject of _____
   a. Very interesting.
   b. Somewhat interesting.
   c. Somewhat uninteresting.
   d. Very uninteresting.

6. List all the subjects you are now taking and then rank-order them from most interesting to least interesting.

There are items (such as Items 7-11) that will bring the student more directly into contact with the subject. Since there may be a difference between what someone says and what he or she does, such "behavioral choice" items are useful. They come closer to requiring a commitment relating to the topic under discussion.

7. If someone suggested that you take up _____ as your life's work, what would you reply?

8. If you were asked to give a short talk about your favorite school subject, which subject would you talk about?

9. What would you reply if, in a casual group discussion, someone said, "_____ is very, very important, and everybody should try to learn as much about it as possible?"

10. Write a paragraph about your favorite school subject. *(Though this is a possible item, it is usually too time-consuming to administer.)*

11. Which of the following subjects would you be most interested in teaching?

    (List your subject and other subjects the student may be studying.)

    a. _____

    b. _____

    c. _____

    d. _____

Another kind of item, generally called the adjective checklist, is shown below. It asks students to circle words that represent their feelings about a subject.

12. Circle each of the words that tell how you feel (mostly) about the subject of _____.

fun	boring	too easy	too hard
useless	useful	exciting	interesting
essential	necessary	worthless	very important

Since it gives the student several quick opportunities to indicate a choice, items modeled after the paired comparison below may also be useful. It is simple to construct. Here's how:

(1) *List your subject and three or four other subjects the student might be currently studying;*

(2) *Make a list of pairs of these subjects, pairing each subject once with every other subject;*

(3) *Reverse the order of some of the pairs so that each subject is listed first about as many times as it is listed second; and*

(4) *Mix up the order of the items.*

With each subject paired at least once with every other subject, the student is asked to consider two subjects at a time and indicate a preference.

For example:

13. On the slips of paper that follow, you are given pairs of subjects. Look at the pairs one at a time and draw a circle around the subject you personally find the more interesting of the two.

1.	algebra	English
2.	history	science
3.	algebra	history
4.	English	science
5.	science	algebra
6.	history	English

A somewhat better index of the student's inclinations is thus gained than if he or she were to comment on each subject by itself. Instructions to the student may vary; they might ask which of the two subjects of a pair the student likes best, which of the two does he or she find more interesting, which of the two would be worth giving up a Saturday afternoon to learn more about, and so on. It is preferable to put each pair of subjects on a separate piece of paper, for later choices might be influenced by the pattern of earlier choices; the student might look back to make sure he or she is "consistent," for example. (A convenient solution is to stack the narrow slips of paper and staple them together on one edge, with one pair of subjects on each slip. This method will make consistency checks more difficult.)

Interpretation of this item is easy, since your interest is confined to a single subject. For each student, count the number of times your subject has been circled. In the above example, each student could circle algebra from zero to three times. If there were 20 students in the class, algebra might be chosen from zero to 60 times, and the "score" might therefore range anywhere from zero to 60. How to interpret the "score"? Well, a "score" near 60 would be as good as you could expect (perfection is an unreasonable expectation), and one near zero should tell you that improvement is possible, that you should ask questions intended to find out why the number isn't larger than it is. Above all, remember that the "score" is nowhere near as precise as the measurement you get from a ruler. Use it as a guide to your next actions, rather than as judgment.

How Long Should a Questionnaire Be?

Your questionnaire should contain as many items as you feel are necessary to give you good evidence about the existence of approach or avoidance tendencies toward your subject.

Which Items Should a Questionnaire Include?

Those that you will accept; those that would cause you to make the instructional changes they suggest. Since you are constructing this instrument for your own use—and *only* for your own use—it makes sense to include only those items that you will accept as meaningful. This is not to say you should not be interested in the *validity* of the items. After all, some items are better indicators than others of how a student is likely to behave in certain situations. But as important as the issue of validity may be, validity should be secondary to self-acceptance. First, develop a set of indicators that you would accept, and *then ask* questions about validity. This way, you can get started now and refine your procedures as you gather experience.

Can You Trust the Responses?

If students know we are asking "attitude" questions, can't they fake their responses? Aren't students merely going to tell us what they think we want to hear?

The honesty with which students will answer the items on a questionnaire depends mainly on how well they trust the person doing the asking. If there is little trust, students will do their best to give what they think are appropriate answers; that is, answers that will do them as little damage as possible. If there is a great deal of trust, students will feel no need to conceal their true opinions, and they will be more likely to respond truthfully.

Suppose I handed out a tendency questionnaire and said, "I am honestly interested in improving my instruction, and I would like very much to know whether I have succeeded in reaching some of my teaching objectives. I'd appreciate it if you would answer these questions as honestly as you can. Your answers will have nothing whatever to do with your grades." And then suppose a small smile turned up my lips in gleeful anticipation. Would you believe my words or my lips?

There are any number of ways in which we can say one thing and clearly communicate something entirely different by our actions, but we *can* get reliable responses to questionnaire items if we ask for responses under appropriate conditions— conditions that convince students that we mean what we say.

If you have been an instructor for any length of time, however, you have probably developed some procedures for administering questionnaires to which there will be only anonymous responses. Perhaps you use items that require checking but no writing. Perhaps you ask a student to collect the papers and shuffle them before handing them to you. These are useful techniques, and you can easily collect others by asking your colleagues. The main thing is to arrange conditions so that students believe their responses will *in no way reflect on them.* Convincing them that there is no way in which you can identify their personal responses may be the best way to succeed. Insist that no names be put on papers, ask a student to collect papers and tabulate responses, ask that the questionnaire be answered outside the classroom and turned in to a student, or ask that papers be put into a box like a voter's ballot box. Whatever procedure you select should indicate to your students your sincerity in wanting to improve the course.

As for instructions to students, I find that I get better results if I tell them I am trying to improve my instruction than if I tell them I am interested in measuring or assessing their attitudes about my subject. Students seem to be more eager to help in response to the first statement than to the second. I asked some students why this might be so, and their answers led me to conclude that it is because the statement "I want to learn something about your attitudes . . ." still has a hint of student grading in it.

What Are They Doing?

Asking people how they feel or how they think they would behave in certain situations is a legitimate way to collect information from which inferences about attitudes may be made. But the adage that says "actions speak louder than words" warrants some thought here. If I tell you that I like to read, and then you discover that I don't own any books and never go to the library, which would you believe—my words or my actions? If I tell you I think comic books are childish, and then you discover that my desk is full of them, would you put more weight on the words or the actions? Right.

All right. If actions speak louder than words, then let's look for action. But not just any action. Let's find out just which actions would satisfy us that our students feel favorably enough about our subject that they will be willing to apply what they've learned. This is a more powerful approach because it focuses directly on desired performances and relieves you of any concern over whether this or that set of performances is or isn't what "favorable attitude" *really* means. You simply describe what student actions would satisfy you, find out how things are going, and then take steps to get more of those actions you consider too infrequent.

Here's how it's done.

1. Describe the things that you would expect students to say or do before you would say they had a favorable attitude toward your subject. Think of someone who does represent the attitude you seek, and list the performances that make you say, "Now *there's* a person with a favorable attitude toward . . ." To help get you started, here's a composite list developed by others. Delete the items that don't apply, and add others that do. Make sure that when your list is finished you can say, "Yes. If students did or said these things, I would say they had a favorable attitude toward my subject."

- ask questions about the subject.
- come early and stay late.
- help other students learn the subject.
- say favorable things about the subject.
- read handouts during breaks.
- ask for more practice.
- practice longer than needed to acquire proficiency.
- ask for related courses.
- encourage others to learn about the subject.
- relate course content to their own job environments.
- do more than the minimum required.
- actually perform the skills being taught.

Again, never mind that some of the items would "fit" better under some category other than "favorable attitude." Just say what you want students to exhibit in the way of "desired performance."

2. When you have finished your draft, make sure that each item on the list is actually something you can see or hear someone do. Then ask yourself this question: "If someone did these things, would I be willing to say that he or she has a favorable attitude toward my subject?" If your answer is yes, then you have completed the list of performances. If your answer is no, then you will need to add the item or items that will cause you to answer in the affirmative.[1]

3. Determine whether each of these actions is occurring to your satisfaction. You can do this by observing whether an action occurs at all, and if it does, count or estimate the frequency with which it occurs. You might also construct a simple questionnaire that asks about each of the actions.

[1] For help with this procedure, see *Goal Analysis,* Third Edition, by R.F. Mager (Center for Effective Performance, Atlanta, GA), 1997.

4. If you find that an action occurs often enough to satisfy you, rejoice. If it does not, you'll want to take steps to find out what you might do to increase the frequency of *that specific action* (without worrying about whether or not it has anything to do with attitude). Suppose, for example, that students are reluctant to ask questions, and you want to decrease that reluctance. Try to find out why they *don't* ask questions. Can it be that they already know the material and don't need further clarification? Or that they're afraid to ask questions for fear of being humiliated? (Think about what happens to students *as a result* of asking a question.)

This procedure will help you learn what is and is not yet happening to your satisfaction and point you in the direction of what to do to get more of what you want. For specific guidance on how to make things better, read on.

11
Improving Results

A poker player down to his last chip was asked, "How're ya doin'?"

"I dunno," he replied.

"What? You don't know how you're making out?"

"Oh, sure," said the player. "I know how I'm making out, but I don't know how I'm doing it."

If we knew what we were doing that was contributing to success, and if we knew what we were doing that was contributing to failure, we could do more of the one and less of the other. After all, we are dripping with good intentions and want only the best for our students. Sometimes, though, we know how well we are doing, but we don't know exactly what to do to improve.

So this chapter is aimed at showing you how to review various components of your instruction in order to spot those components that may be acting to dampen the enthusiasm of your students. The purpose is to show you how to spot unproductive practices that may have sneaked onto the scene while you weren't looking; the purpose is to identify opportunities for improvement. Once you know what they are, you will know what to do: *Weaken the negatives and strengthen the positives.* You may not have the clout to do anything about some of them, but you will know what should be done about them.

Affect Analysis

The procedure I'll describe has to do with analyzing those conditions and consequences that influence *affect*—that is, the approach/avoidance tendencies related to the subject you are teaching. It isn't difficult to do, but that doesn't make doing it any less important.

Specifically, the procedure asks you to answer three main questions:

1. Are there obstacles that make it harder than necessary for students to come into contact with the subject? In other words, is it somehow difficult for students to get to the place where the subject is being taught or difficult to get the materials they need?

2. Are there unpleasant or aversive conditions associated with *being* in contact with the subject? Is it somehow uncomfortable or humiliating to study the subject?

3. Are there unpleasant or aversive consequences experienced by students as a *result* of coming into contact with your subject? Are students somehow made to feel smaller as a result of studying or applying what they have learned?

Some Examples

Sometimes the conditions and consequences that get in the way of more positive feelings toward the subject are easy to spot; actually, most are easy to spot once you initiate the hunt.

Occasionally, they are more devious. Here are some examples:

Example #1

When I had occasion to teach Introductory Psychology more than 200 years ago, the other faculty members and I knew exactly what incoming students were interested in. They were interested in sex, in hypnotism, in ESP, and in the antics of the weird person living down the hall of the dormitory. We knew all that. We talked about it, and we agreed on it. So how did we start the course? Did we tug on these interests and help them blossom to even greater heights? Did we fan these interests so that we could stimulate interest in other topics as well? Not for a minute! We started with the *history* of psychology. We bored the pants off these eager students with stories of the early eighteenth century, and about how . . . ZZZZZZZzzz. (Stop it! You're putting me to sleep.)

And then we would sit around in the faculty lounge complaining about the attitude of these students. Good grief. One should *never* begin teaching a subject to newcomers by teaching the history of the subject. That's the last thing students care about *at that point*. There's no *reason* for them to care. First, teach them something related to their interests; then, give them some skill in the area . . . along with feelings of competence. Do that, and then—because studying a subject's history is one way of fondling the subject, one way of getting closer to it—students may later *become* interested in the subject's history.

Example #2

A smashing example of the *right* way to begin a course was found in a locksmithing course I took by correspondence, after sending in an ad I found in a magazine. It was apparent that the developers of this course knew exactly why their students were taking this course, just as we knew why our students were taking our psychology courses. People were interested in knowing how to pick a lock. So guess where the course started. Right. Lesson 1 was on how to pick a lock. No history, no preamble; just a lesson on the subject most interesting *at that time* to the entering student. Nobody had to tell students that they weren't experts just because they knew how to pick one little lock; it was perfectly obvious. But oh, what a difference it made in attitude toward the subject! I was eager for the next lesson. Then I discovered that each set of five lessons came in a carton containing about two dozen numbered brown envelopes, about 2 x 3 inches, sealed. When, in the middle of a lesson, I was told "Now open Envelope 23," I would eagerly tear it open. Maybe it was only a key blank or an Allen wrench, but opening the envelope was better than eating peanuts.

In fact, the course was laid out in such an attitude-enhancing manner that I found myself writing an irate letter to my instructor . . . because I had run out of lessons before the next batch had arrived. Now *that's* how to organize a course to improve attitude toward the subject.

Example #3

As I said earlier, it isn't always easy to spot the conditions or consequences acting against you (such as teaching the history of a subject before teaching the subject itself). I once had occasion to conduct an affect analysis for a teacher who couldn't understand the difficulty she was having in her class. She was a fourth-grade art teacher who was very successful in motivating an interest in art activities. She was liked by her students, and they wanted to be able to do the things she could do. But by mid-semester it became clear that interest in art was declining. Many of the children demonstrated increasing apathy toward art and began expressing antagonism toward art class (not toward the teacher, but toward "art *class*"). An affect analysis for this teacher revealed the somewhat subtle cause of this situation. In explaining the project for the day, the teacher used between one-fourth and one-half of the class period. Then, just as the children had organized their materials and were hard at work, the bell rang and they had to stop and go on to another classroom.

There was good motivation in this case and an enthusiastic and skillful teacher. But there was also an event that successfully blocked the motivated activity of the students . . . and frustration resulted. Since frustration is one of the conditions people try to avoid, these students came to associate art class with something unpleasant. Aggravating the situation still further was the fact that the teacher knew time was short, and this caused her to hover over the students and urge them to work faster.

Once this state of affairs was pointed out to the teacher, there was no need to suggest a solution; making her aware of it was enough. Although she had no control over the length of the period and could not change the administrative rules, she was able to get around the restrictive time allocation by reorganizing her activities so more work time (and less teacher-talk time) would be available to the students.

Example #4

Here is an example of how a single situation can make it both difficult to come into contact with a subject and unpleasant to be in contact with it. During one college semester I took a course in a subject that I had looked forward to for some time. But this class was held in a building at the other end of the campus from my previous class. Because we had only ten minutes to get from one class to another, I had to run to get to the second class. Needless to say, I arrived in a sweat and then had to sit through the next class in sweaty (translation: smelly) condition. It was uncomfortable, and it made it difficult to concentrate on the subject at hand.

Example #5

Some years ago, a company that manufactured telephone equipment decided to modernize its training establishment. The first step was to get rid of the ancient lecture-in-the-morning, lab-in-the-afternoon format. This meant that instead of classrooms and labs (where the practicing was done), they would have only combination classroom-labs.

Once reconfigured, each room housed the lab equipment on which students would practice. In addition, there were places where trainees could sit and study, or they could gather around when the instructor wanted to spend a few minutes explaining a concept or demonstrating a procedure.

This arrangement made it easy for students to come into contact with the subject matter, and their interest in the subject, as well as their willingness to work harder, soared. Other companies have since adopted this student-friendly way of organizing the instructional space.

Example #6

Here's an example of an instance in which the consequence of showing an interest in a subject (an approach response) was punished. During an experiment on learner-controlled instruction, one of the engineer/students asked a question of the engineer/instructor. The instructor, who was always interested in answering questions in a thoughtful way, responded in his usual fashion. He walked up to the student, scowled, tugged at his eyebrow, and lifted one foot off the floor. This is what he did when he was thinking. But the student didn't know the meaning of this strange behavior. The result? The session recording showed that the student never volunteered another word for fifty-three minutes. (When the instructor was made aware of his intimidating pose, he immediately vowed to give it up in favor of a more pleasant demeanor. And he did, too.)

Example #7

Because so many computer manuals are still written from the subject matter's, rather than from the user's, point of view, it is more difficult than necessary to find the information needed to eliminate an already frustrating work stoppage. Ask a computer user why he or she doesn't look to the manual and you're likely to hear, "Arrgh! I'd rather ask my cube-mate; it's a lot faster."

What to Observe

When hunting for conditions and consequences that may be getting in the way of a more favorable attitude, or stronger self-efficacy, there are five general areas to explore:

1. The physical environment.
2. The instructional materials and equipment.
3. The instructor.
4. The instructional procedures.
5. Administration policies.

Within each of these areas, you will be interested in looking for opportunities to:

1. Make it easier for students to actually get to the subject matter, to initiate the learning process;
2. Make it less aversive and more comfortable to be in the presence of the subject matter and of the learning process itself; and
3. Make the consequences of learning and of student eagerness to demonstrate their growing competence as positive as possible.

How to Do It

To make it easier to spot opportunities for improvement in the five areas, I've provided an Attitude Checklist that appears on the following pages. Though the questions on the Checklist

will suggest what to do to find the answers, here is a short set
of general guidelines on how to proceed:

1. Look around your learning environment while answering the questions in Section I of the Checklist.

2. Inspect the instructional materials and actually operate the equipment while answering the questions in Section II of the Checklist.

3. Video-record one or two of your class sessions. If you have lab sessions, discussion sessions, role-play sessions, etc., record one or two of them, too. If you think you can handle it emotionally, put a video camera at the *front* of the classroom pointed at the *students*. That will show you how students are reacting as you present material.

    Review the recordings in private while answering the questions in Sections III and IV of the Checklist.

4. Answer the questions in Section V of the Checklist.

5. Ask a few of your students whether they are experiencing any obstacles to learning. You might give them a copy of the Checklist to prod their thinking.

ATTITUDE CHECKLIST

The items on this Checklist should help you identify changes that will make it easier for students to feel favorably toward what they are learning. If you find yourself placing a check mark in the "?" column, ask a student.

I. Physical Environment	Yes	?	No	Comments
1. Are the classrooms open during the times when students prefer to study?				
2. Do students have adequate work space?				
3. Is the student work space relatively comfortable?				
4. Is the environment too hot? Too cold? Too noisy? Too stuffy?				
5. Do students need to travel long distances to get to the classroom?				
6. Is it easy for them to get to the classroom?				
7. Are students often called away from the classroom?				
8. Can students easily *see* and *hear* the instruction?				
9. Is the lighting good?				
10. Are students allowed to move freely around the learning environment, rather than bolted to the floor in rows?				
11. May students leave the classroom to take care of personal needs?				
12. Are there avoidable distractions? Noise? Activity?				
13. Is there tension, either deliberate or accidental?				
14. Are students anxious to leave the learning environment?				
15. Are students relieved when they leave the learning environment?				
16. Do students find excuses to leave the environment?				

II. Instructional Materials and Devices	Yes	?	No	Comments
1. Is it easy to hear and see the instructor?				
2. Are the materials easy to get at?				
3. Is the reading difficulty appropriate for the students?				
4. Is it easy to see the place or importance of the materials; do students consider them useful?				
5. Are the materials relevant to the learning objectives?				
6. Are the instructional materials interesting?				
7. Are there materials that help the student learn the subject in addition to the instructor's words *about* the subject?				
8. Do type size and style make it difficult to read the material? (Ask a student.)				
9. Is the material organized so that the student can easily find what he or she is looking for? Is it clearly indexed?				
10. Are computer terminals or other equipment available when students need or want them?				
11. Can the equipment be operated easily? Extension cords available?				
12. Is the sound quality of audio materials good enough so that students can hear with ease?				
13. Does the equipment work reliably?				
14. When the equipment breaks down, is there someone there to repair it within a reasonable time?				
15. Are additional supplies (paper, pencils, etc.) readily available?				

III. Instructor	Yes	?	No	Comments
Does the instructor:				
1. Speak loudly enough for all to hear easily?				
2. Speak clearly?				
3. Use a vocabulary level consistent with the subject level? (Does he or she use a freshman vocabulary for freshman subjects?)				
4. Continually orient students so that they always know where they are and where they are going?				
5. Specify instructional objectives clearly? Give students written copies of the objectives?				
6. Allow or encourage questions?				
7. Allow or encourage discussion and allow students to express and develop their own ideas?				
8. Allow or encourage students to pursue some special interest they may have developed in the subject?				
9. Avoid putting students to sleep with a monotone?				
10. Avoid distracting students with annoying mannerisms; e.g., swaying back and forth while lecturing; repeatedly uttering the same phrases, such as "Right?" or "You know what I mean?"; speech mannerisms such as er..ah..um.				
11. Avoid reading the textbook aloud?				
12. Devote minimum time to lecturing?				
13. Avoid rambling?				
14. Appear to be interested or enthusiastic about the subject? How much so?				

III. Instructor (cont.)	Yes	?	No	Comments
Does the instructor:				
15. Avoid requiring students to remain inactive for long periods of time?				
16. Show interest in teaching students, rather than merely keeping order?				
17. Behave as he or she wants each student to behave?				
18. Generate discomfort while talking about or presenting the subject?				
19. Encourage students who are eager to demonstrate their achievement, rather than frighten them or make them anxious?				
20. Respond to student questions?				
21. Answer student questions with interest rather than hostility, insult, ridicule, or disdain?				
22. Respond to student comments or attempts to discuss the subject?				
23. Respond when a student completes a project or turns in an assignment? How?				
24. Return exam results promptly?				
25. Treat student work with respect, rather than hold the work up to ridicule?				
26. Insist that projects or assignments be evaluated promptly? By whom?				
27. Use subject matter as an instrument of punishment?				
28. Insist that assignments be turned in promptly, and then ignore them?				
29. Do anything that convinces the student that he or she could never become competent in the subject? That his or her best efforts aren't good enough?				

IV. Instructional Procedures	Yes	?	No	Comments
1. Do students have a clear idea of what they will be expected to be able to do at the end of the instruction?				
2. Is each student provided with a copy of the objectives at the beginning of the instruction?				
3. Does each student have a copy of the course procedures (the rules by which the course will be conducted)?				
4. Are students required to show up at a certain time and prevented from studying before that time?				
5. Are all students expected to study the same thing at the same time and for the same length of time? (i.e., must they all proceed at the same rate?)				
6. Do the rules make it difficult for students to study a topic when they feel interested in it?				
7. Is the instructor accessible to the students when needed?				
8. Does distance get between students and the subject? How far do students have to travel between the classroom and laboratory? Between classrooms?				
9. Are materials accessible to each student when he/she needs them?				
10. Is the library open when each student is free to use it?				
11. Are library books easily accessible to the student? Are you sure the librarian does not stand between the student and the books?				
12. Is there paperwork (form-filling) between the student and library books?				

IV. Instructional Procedures (cont.)	Yes	?	No	Comments
13. Is there administrative procedure between the instructor and course materials?				
14. Is equipment permanently available where students can use it?				
15. Are films, videotapes, and computer software permanently available where students can use them?				
16. Are students allowed to operate the equipment?				
17. Are visuals permanently available where the instructor uses them?				
18. Does the student spend too great a portion of the period setting up and taking down equipment? Signing in and out?				
19. Are students encouraged rather than discouraged?				
20. Are brighter students prevented from "getting ahead" of slower students?				
21. Are slower students given time to understand the subject?				
22. Are students of considerably differing abilities paired, causing boredom to the faster and frustration or embarrassment to the slower?				

A "Yes" response to Items 1–5 points to an opportunity for improvement.

V. Administrative Policy	Yes	?	No	Comments
1. Must students turn off their interest in one subject when a rigid time block ends (the bell rings) and turn on their interest in another subject? In other words, must student interest conform to administrative policy? Does policy discourage students from working with a subject until they reach a stopping point?				
2. Are classes frequently interrupted by announcements over a PA system or by other intrusions?				
3. Are there conditions that make it difficult for the instructor to maintain interest in his or her students and in the subject?				
4. Is the instructor overloaded with busy work?				
5. Are students who finish their work earlier than others made to sit still until the period is over? Is their diligence followed by some other form of unpleasant consequence, such as cleaning chores or "make work" assignments? ("Since you finished early, you can go out and whitewash those rocks.")				
6. Are grades based on individual student's achievement in relation to course objectives? In other words, is evaluation based on objective-related performance?				
7. Is there recognition or privileges for student achievement?				
8. Do instructors hand out at least as many rewards as punishments?				

V. Administrative Policy (cont.)	Yes	?	No	Comments
9. Regarding the kinds of instructor performance that management rewards: are instructors rewarded on the basis of their interest in, and efforts on behalf of, students? Are instructors rewarded on the basis of the amount of student behavior they have changed? (Are you sure they are not rewarded mostly for committee work, publications, and the amount of equipment they display?)				
10. Does administrative policy *allow* successful instructors to be rewarded more than unsuccessful ones?				
11. Does administrative policy reward unsuccessful teaching by taking from the classroom those students with whom the teacher has failed and giving them to specialists to work with in remote locations?				
12. Do managers take steps to identify how well each instructor is performing?				

What to Do Next

Now that you've collected some information about conditions and consequences that students may consider less than desirable, what should you do about it? That may sound like a silly question, but it isn't, because there are any number of ways you might proceed. Here are my suggestions about what to do—suggestions that will give you the quickest improvement in student attitude for the least amount of effort.

1. Make sure you understand the information you have collected. If you checked any items in the question-mark columns, it means you aren't sure of how to respond to those particular items. Remedy? Ask a student or two how they would respond to the items.

2. Review your responses. Circle every check you made (either in the "Yes" column or the "No" column) that indicates an opportunity for *improvement*. For example, under Section I, a "No" in response to question 2 indicates an opportunity for improvement and should be circled; whereas a "Yes" to question 4 means improvement is needed.

3. Now examine these items that represent opportunities for improvement. Your first move should be to do something about the item that is *easiest* to change. This item may not be the action that will make the biggest improvement, but it will be quick and easy to deal with, and it will help you feel good about making some progress.

   For example, if there are distractions that you can eliminate, that would be a good place to begin. Eliminate visitors or keep the visit frequency to an absolute minimum. Have students turn off their beepers. Tell them not to bring their cellular phones to class. Put a sign on your classroom door that says "Singapore" or "London," so that when someone tries to pry one of your students out of the classroom, you can honestly say, "Sorry; she's in London."

4. One by one, try to do something about the other items that need attention, continuing to make the easiest fix of those remaining. You will find, maybe to your surprise, that you have control over a large number of the needed changes; there will be only a few instances in which you will need either the cooperation or permission of others to remove the obstacle.

5. When you've done all you can, then try to do something about those items over which you have little or no control. Badger the people in charge of keeping the equipment in working order; try to order items that will make your instructional operation work more smoothly.

6. Finally, review the items you did not circle. These describe practices that you are doing right. Look at each item and ask yourself whether it would be possible to make it even "righter" (the editor will kill me for that).

    For example, if you have derived the objectives for your instruction from a real need and let your students in on the secret of what they are expected to accomplish, you are doing a good thing. If, however, you haven't yet provided each student with a copy of those objectives at the beginning of the instruction, doing so will be an even better move toward sending students away with a more favorable attitude.

As you can see, the quest for attitude-enhancing practices is a never-ending process of successive approximations. Happily, the process involves skills that you already own. All you have to do is put them to use.

Summing Up

Our attitudes are influenced by the things that happen to us. When good things happen to us while in the presence of another person, we tend to feel more favorable toward that person. When we are made to feel smaller in the presence of that person, we tend to avoid future contact.

The same is true for the subjects we teach. By neglecting student feeling, we can send them away with wrinkled attitudes toward our subject; we can send them away with a tendency to avoid the subject whenever they can. But by making sure that being in the presence of the subject makes them feel good about themselves, by making sure that the results of being in the presence of the subject make them feel good about themselves, by making sure that we model the enthusiasm we would like to encourage, we can send students away feeling good about what they were taught and showing eagerness to learn more.

It isn't difficult. And it's well worth doing.

12
An Awesome Power

As we have seen in this book, people influence people . . . whether they want to or not. That's easy to understand. What may be less apparent is that the *degree* to which they influence others can be awesome to behold. Not only is it possible to influence attitude and self-efficacy for better or worse, it is possible to cause people with mediocre skills to excel, or to destroy the exceptional. Therefore, the importance of how we behave toward others cannot be overestimated. Let me show you just how powerful your actions can be.

We begin by asking ourselves these questions: "What is it that makes Mozart, Joe Montana, Jascha Heifetz, or Arnold Palmer different from the rest of us? Why are they light years beyond the rest of us in the skills with which they apply their specialties? And how did they get that way?"

The common belief, of course, is that high levels of proficiency are the result of "gifts" or of heredity, rather than of experience and practice. You hear people say, "Of course Itzhak Perlman is a super musician. He was born with a silver violin in his mouth." Or "Joe Montana is a superstar because he inherited an enormous talent for football."

But conclusions such as these are the result of superstitious thinking; i.e., if you can't see the cause, attribute it to magic. And if you can attribute it to magic, then you don't have to accept any responsibility at all for your own shortcomings. In other words, if you believe that the super-proficient got that way because of forces beyond their control, then you can tell yourself that there's nothing you can ever do to become like them. You can tell yourself things such as, "I could never learn math," or "I could never be good at public speaking." After all, if you weren't born with the skill, there's nothing you can do to acquire it. (Phootnote: "Talent" is not the same as skill. Skill is an actual ability to do something; "talent" is part of the raw material from which skill may be developed.)

A comfy way to look at the issue, I admit, but wrong. Research results suggest that superstars are *made,* not born. What? How can that be, when everyone knows that "child prodigies" show their excellence at a very early age? How can superstars be made, when some of them have been known to write operas when barely out of their diapers? And if superstars are made, how come we don't make more of them?

To be sure, superstars usually begin with a good dose of talent, but talent is by no means enough. Unless certain things happen, the talent doesn't blossom into skill. Besides, very few child prodigies ever grow up to be adult prodigies. Now why do you suppose that is? Is it because the pool of "talent" was finite and just ran out? Because the "gift" simply evaporated into thin air?

On the one hand, then, we have child prodigies who lose it before adulthood. On the other hand, there are child prodigies who just keep getting better and better as they become adults, and there are people with ordinary talent who have been made into superstars. Consider the work of Shinichi Suzuki, a well-known Japanese musician who gave violin lessons to gymnasiums full of students. A review of Suzuki's students shows that many who began taking violin lessons from him *without any signs of musical talent* attained levels of skill comparable to musical prodigies. What? Students with no obvious talent turning into super-proficient musicians? How is such a thing possible if they weren't born with the "gift"? How indeed? Suzuki's explanation (from his later writings) was that ". . . every child can become highly educated if he is given the proper training." Hear that? His message was that training can make light-years of difference in the level of skill that can be acquired, even among those without a special "gift." *But it has to be the proper kind of training!*

There's even more evidence to support the thesis that superstars are made, not born. A few musicians are blessed with absolute pitch—commonly referred to as "perfect pitch." Play any note, and they can tell you what that note is. Wow! What a "gift." But wait a minute. Research has shown that absolute pitch appears as a consequence of appropriate musical instruction and ample opportunities to interact with a musical instrument. That is, those with perfect pitch had the "right" kind of training and the "right" opportunities to interact with a musical instrument. But here's the interesting part. Absolute pitch can be acquired by anyone, but only if they are between the ages of three and five. But so what? If kids can be taught a skill commonly thought to be the result of a special "gift," then we know that this "superskill" is teachable—regardless of "gift."

Now if anyone between the ages of three and five can acquire perfect pitch, why is it so rare? The answer lies in the definition of "right" kind of training and opportunity. (By the way, most musicians with perfect pitch find it extremely annoying: to them, everybody else is off-key.)

Am I trying to tell you that there is no such thing as a child prodigy or that one person isn't born with more innate "talent" than another? No, no, not at all. But prodigies follow the same sequence of skill-development stages as everybody else. The main difference is that they attain higher levels faster and at earlier ages. For example, Picasso's earlier drawings show that he mastered the same problems the same way as the less gifted do—just faster. Like Picasso, other superstars make the same mistakes and have to solve the same problems as the less talented—they just go through the bumbling stages a lot faster than you or I might.

So if ordinary people can become adult prodigies, how come there aren't more of them? One researcher (Feldman, 1980) answers that question this way: Prodigious performance is rare because extreme talent for a specific activity in a particular child and the necessary environmental support and instruction rarely coincide.

In other words, the number of super-performers might be increased if they could experience the right mix of environmental and training conditions.

How It Happens

Well now, if there is a way to make superstars out of ordinary people and a way for child prodigies to keep from losing their talent, just what are the ingredients of the magic potion by which this is accomplished?

The research summarized from the report quoted above ("Expert Performance," by K. Anders & Neil Chamess: *The American Psychologist*, August, 1994) included several tantalizing conclusions; for example, that many child prodigies don't grow up to be adult prodigies, that many people of ordinary talent grow into exceptional performers, and that people of all levels of talent are shorn of their potential by the conditions and consequences with which they happen to be surrounded. The question that remains is, "Just how do exceptional performers get to be that way?" How do child prodigies get to be adult prodigies, and how do people of "ordinary talent" become prodigious performers? It happens like this:

The process begins at an early age with play. Children try this and that (e.g., mud pies, mandolins, pianos), thus gaining experience with various aspects of their environment. If the play is an enjoyable experience—and if the play isn't punished—they'll get better at it, and one parent or another will ultimately notice "talent."

"Hey. This kid's got talent," they will say and then arrange for the child to take lessons. That initiates deliberate, but limited, practice, with a source of individual coaching, feedback, and reinforcement. It is these conditions—supervised practice, with feedback and reinforcement—that provide the key to development of expert performance.

While this is going on, the parents help the child (help, not nag) to acquire regular practice habits. The parents teach the child that practice has instrumental (practical) value in that practice leads to increments of improvement. The parents point out and reinforce these increments of improvement (e.g., "You handled that movement a lot more smoothly today than you did yesterday."). At the same time, they refrain from dwelling on shortcomings (e.g., "You really look butt-heavy when you skate backward") or comparisons of the child's performance with that of a superstar (e.g., "You've still got a long way to go before you're another Michael Jordan") or such inspiring comments as "I always *knew* you'd never amount to anything."

The next phase begins when the child decides to turn what started as play into a full-time activity. Daily practice periods are then vastly increased, and as the practice leads to visibly improved performance, more advanced teachers are sought out. Improving performance leads to favorable recognition and praise by those other than parents and coaches, and the activity itself takes on rewarding properties; i.e., "doing it" becomes its own reward. Practice becomes self-perpetuating because of the joy experienced by engaging in the activity.

One of two things finally happens. Either the student decides he or she can, and will, make a living at the activity or decides to continue the activity as a hobby or avocation only.

So what begins as enjoyable play ends as enjoyable, highly skilled, productive activity.

It is important to note that *practice alone is not enough* for the creation of superstar performers. No less critical is the careful orchestration (either accidental or deliberate) of environmental and social factors. The opportunity to practice must be readily available (e.g., there's a piano in the house and the child is allowed to use it), and the environment must provide positive reinforcement for practice and improvement (i.e., someone says favorable things about the activity and its results).

To understand why so many people never get to grow whatever talent to the point of expert performance, re-read the previous paragraph. It's because opportunities for deliberate practice are lacking and because the consequences of practice are unpleasant or painful (e.g., hearing "You know you'll never amount to anything," or any of the thousands of other disparaging remarks and acts that can squash forever the motivation to continue). What makes the difference isn't the size of the talent so much as the predisposition to deliberate practice over many years, a predisposition nurtured by a supportive environment.

The tragedy is that if you poke your head out your window, you can almost hear the screams from the ocean of talent being incinerated by thoughtless parents showering disparaging remarks on their offspring and at the same time making sure that practice is anything but an enjoyable event (e. g., "Just for *that*, you can practice *twice* as long today!").

The encouraging fact is that it is within the power of each and every one of us to assist in providing just the kind of environment that will lead to opposite results; that is, instead of slashing deliberately or accidentally at a growing talent, to provide the kind of fertile "soil" in which that person, as well as the talent within, can grow to greater and greater heights.

Though we do not, and cannot, control all the components from which nurturing environments are created, we must accept the responsibility to act in the best interest of those we serve—to help them grow rather than to shrivel. After all, there are enough aversion-producing forces in this old world of ours. As professionals, we must not let it be said that we are among them.

Epilogue

It is easy to teach avoidance . . . anywhere in the world you look there is evidence of that. As a species, we do not seem to lack skill in teaching each other to avoid people of other colors, of other ideas, of other religions, and those who might have been born in this country or that. Perhaps there is something about us that makes this inevitable . . . perhaps we are not yet civilized enough, or strong enough, to apply what is already known in preventing further spread of aversion. Perhaps it isn't realistic for us to believe we are ready to try to stamp out the game of "you name it and I'll teach you to avoid it."

Perhaps.

Be that as it may, those with the responsibility for influencing the performance of others cannot accept such a defeatist position. To be a professional means to accept responsibility . . . responsibility for actions and for results. It is to act in the best interests of those served . . . to help them grow rather than shrivel. When we accept the responsibility for professionally influencing the lives and actions of other people, we must do all we can to make that influence positive rather than negative. When we accept the money and the trust of the community, we must accept not only the responsibility for sending our students away with as much knowledge and skill as is within our power to give them, but also for sending them away with the ability and the inclination to use those skills to help themselves and others.

There are enough aversion-producing instruments in this old world of ours. We must not let it be said that we are among them.

A Time for Tribute

"Help, help," I cried. And did they ever!

As you might guess, a book about approach tendencies ought to trigger approach responses toward the subject of approach responses. Accordingly, *How to Turn Learners On . . . without turning them off* was formulated in two loose stages. The first stage consisted of telling the content to members of the intended audience, individually and in groups, and noting their reactions, comments, and suggestions. The object was to find out what it took to get them nodding and to keep them nodding all the way through. (But not nodding off.)

The second stage began when the content was in written form. It consisted mainly of asking instructors and colleagues who tested the various drafts to mark anything that slowed them down, turned them off, or rubbed them the wrong way; to describe what might have caused them to back off; and finally, to describe what might have caused them to move forward.

And did they ever!

They made me change the sequence of topics until it made sense to *them,* and showed no respect whatever for what was "logical" to *me;* ripped out paragraphs I was very fond of and trampled them into oblivion; caused the demise of clever explanations that nobody seemed to understand; bludgeoned me into burning a long chapter (indeed!) on the development of affective objectives (there's no such thing) and half of one on the statistics of attitude assessment (nobody cared); and vetoed examples that didn't examp.

Such impudence cannot go unpunished; such ego batterers must be exposed to public view. Therefore, with ropes of gratitude I tie to the pillory of immortality the 30 teachers who attended the workshop sponsored by the London County Council, the 20 teachers who attended a workshop sponsored by the University of Buffalo, the nine graduate student-teachers of the University of Rochester; and these original culprits, who made marks all over my neat pages:

Albert Bandura; Bruce Bergum; Edith Bryant; David Cram; Anne Dreyfuss; Sister Charlene Foster, S.N.D. de Namur; Arthur Hyatt; Jane Kilkenny; Leon Lessinger; Richard Lewis; Jeanne Mager; Mike Nisos; Judy Opfer; Peter Pipe; Maryjane Rees; Charles Selden; Nancy Selden; Caroline Smiley; Margaret Steen; James Straubel; Walter Thorne; and Jack Vaughn. Especially in need of public exposure are those who offered their artistic opinion and witty remarks regarding cover design drafts. And those are these: Johan Adriaanse, Gérard Conesa, Paul Guersch, David Heath, Eileen Mager, Clair Miller, Fahad Omair, Dan Piskorik, Phil Postel, Jim Reed, Ethel Robinson, Bill Valen, Carol Valen, Bob White, and Letitia Wiley.

Not to be outdone, there were those who couldn't resist sloshing around in the present edition, gleefully pointing to lumps and potholes needing my attention. Folks such as these cannot be allowed to point and snicker behind a veil of anonymity, so expose them I will: **David Cram, Kay Newell, Dan Lansell, Eileen Mager,** and **Verne Niner.** Finally, I must reveal that Mary Kitzmiller was the kindly (!) editress whose sharp eyes and red pencil smoothed the grammatical bumps and tangles.

With music swelling in the background, I raise my glass to all in a burst of thanks and appreciation for their insightful efforts.

RFM

Index

MORE GREAT BOOKS FROM DR. ROBERT F. MAGER!

Dr. Robert F. Mager has authored one of the most extensive and renowned collections of books and resources on issues of human performance in existence today. These books are considered to be *the* reference library for anyone serious about educating others and improving human performance. You'll find everything you need to learn how to:

- develop successful instruction,
- find realistic solutions to performance problems,
- measure the results of your instruction,
- generate positive attitudes in learners,
- and much more!

Order your copies today and get resources you'll use for a lifetime.

	Quantity	x Price=	Total
Measuring Instructional Results *How to determine whether your instructional results have been achieved*		x $19.95=	
Preparing Instructional Objectives *A critical tool in the development of effective instruction*		x $19.95=	
How to Turn Learners On... without turning them off *Ways to ignite interest in learning*		x $19.95=	
Analyzing Performance Problems *How to figure out why people aren't doing what they should be, and what to do about it*		x $19.95=	
Making Instruction Work *A step-by-step guide to designing and developing instruction that works*		x $19.95=	
Goal Analysis *How to clarify your goals so you can actually achieve them*		x $19.95=	
The How to Write a Book Book		x $17.95=	
Troubleshooting the Troubleshooting Course		x $17.95=	
What Every Manager Should Know About Training		x $17.95=	
Subtotal			
Shipping & Handling*			
GA residents add 5% sales tax to the subtotal plus shipping and handling			
Total Order			

* Please add $4.50 for the first book, plus $1.50 for each additional book. Please allow four weeks for delivery by UPS Ground Service.

Name _____

Phone _____ Fax _____

Organization _____

Address _____

City _____ State _____ Zip _____

- My check or money order for $ _____is enclosed

Charge my • Visa • Mastercard • AmEx   Exp. Date _____

Card Number _____

Name on Card _____

Please send this form and your check, money order, or credit card number to:

CEP
P.O. Box 102462
Atlanta, GA 30368-2462

Call 1-800-558-4CEP for volume discount information.

Call for shipping charges on international orders.

For credit card orders, fax this order for faster delivery: (770) 458-9109